DINOSAUR
COLORING BOOKS FOR KIDS

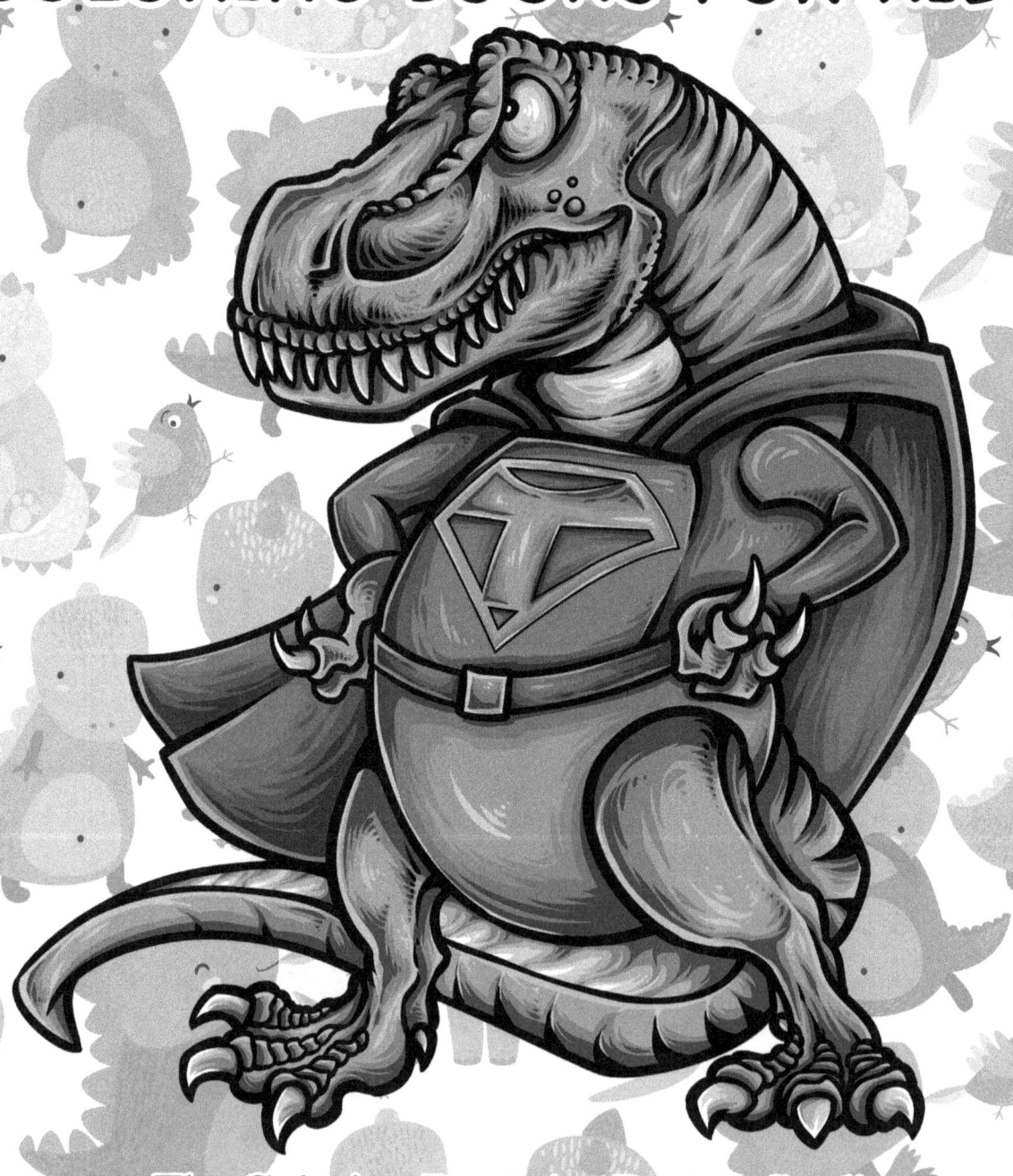

The Coloring Book Art Design Studio

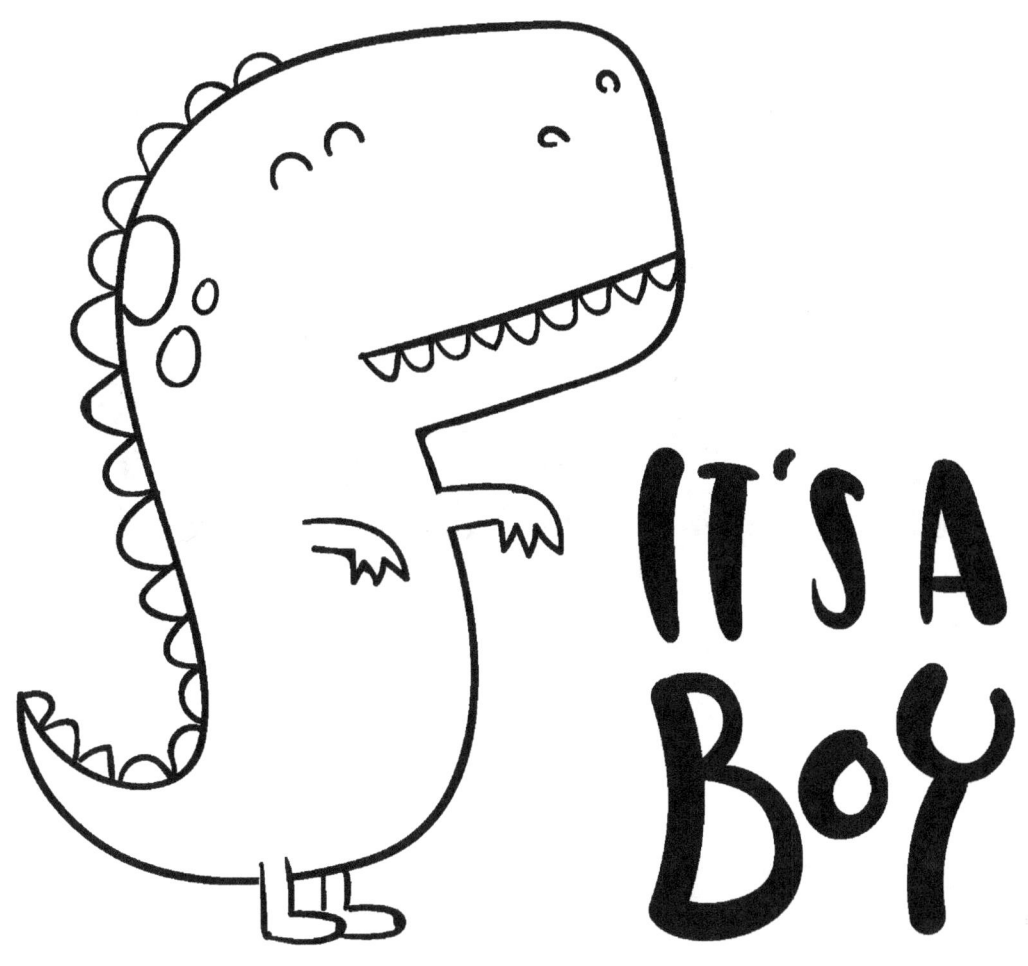

DINOSAUR
COLORING BOOKS FOR KIDS

by The Coloring Book Art Design Studio

DINOSAUR
COLORING BOOKS FOR KIDS

Copyright © 2018 by The Coloring Book Art Design Studio

All rights reserved. No part of this publication may be reproduced, distributed, or transmitted in any form or by any means, including photocopying, recording, or other electronic or mechanical methods, without the prior written permission of the publisher, except in the case of brief quotations embodied in critical reviews and certain other noncommercial uses permitted by copyright law.

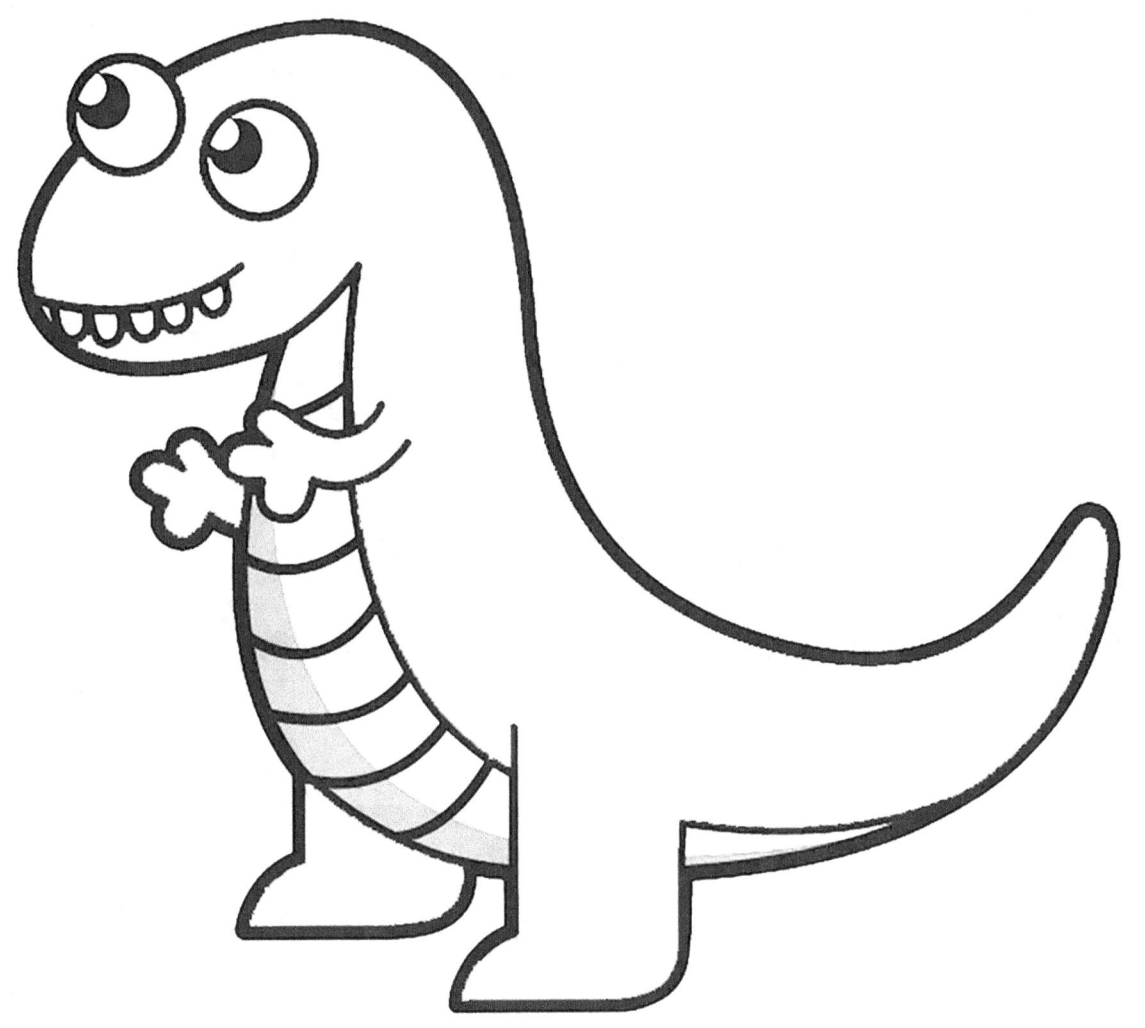

THIS BOOK
BELONG TO

_____

_____

LET'S TEST YOUR COLOR

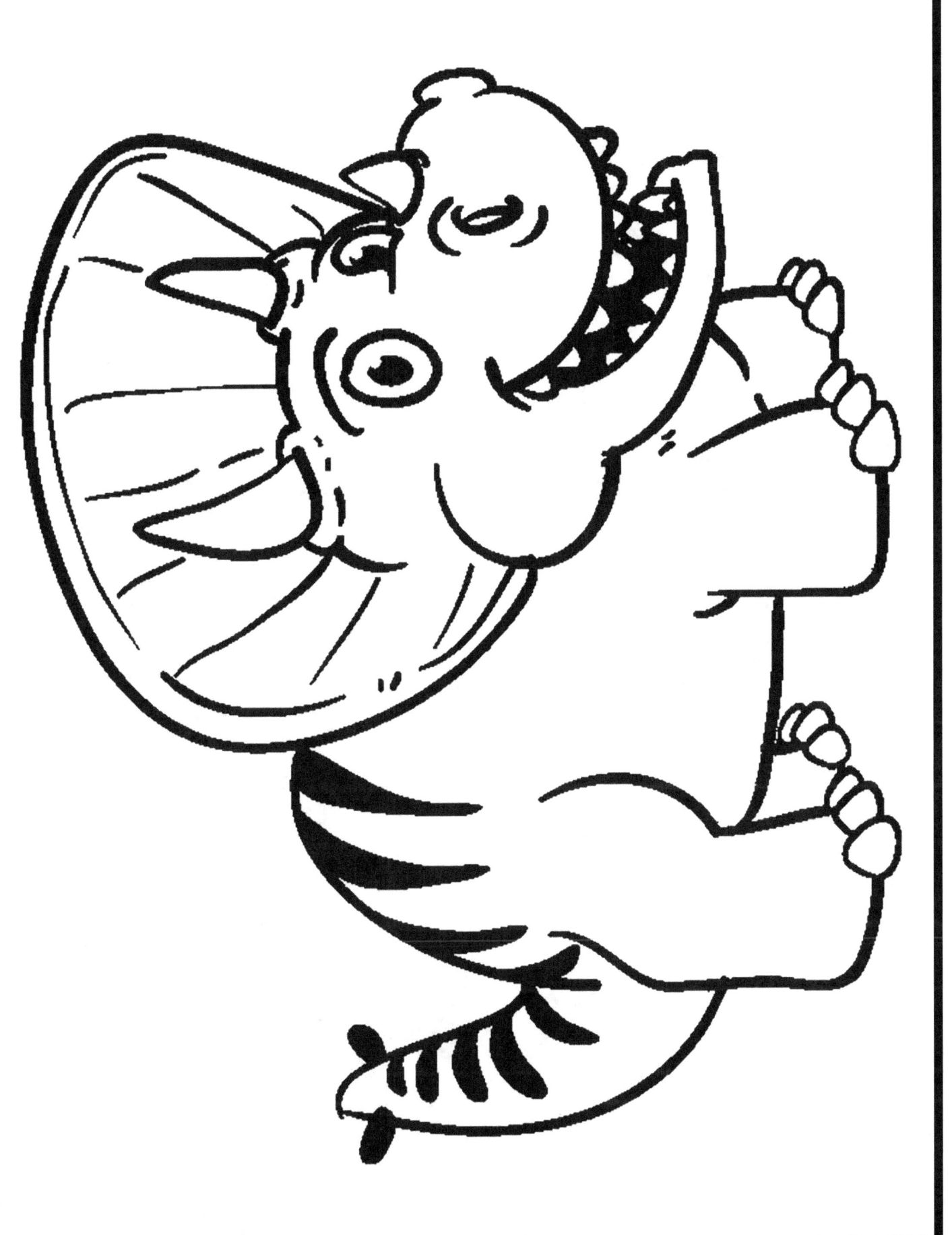

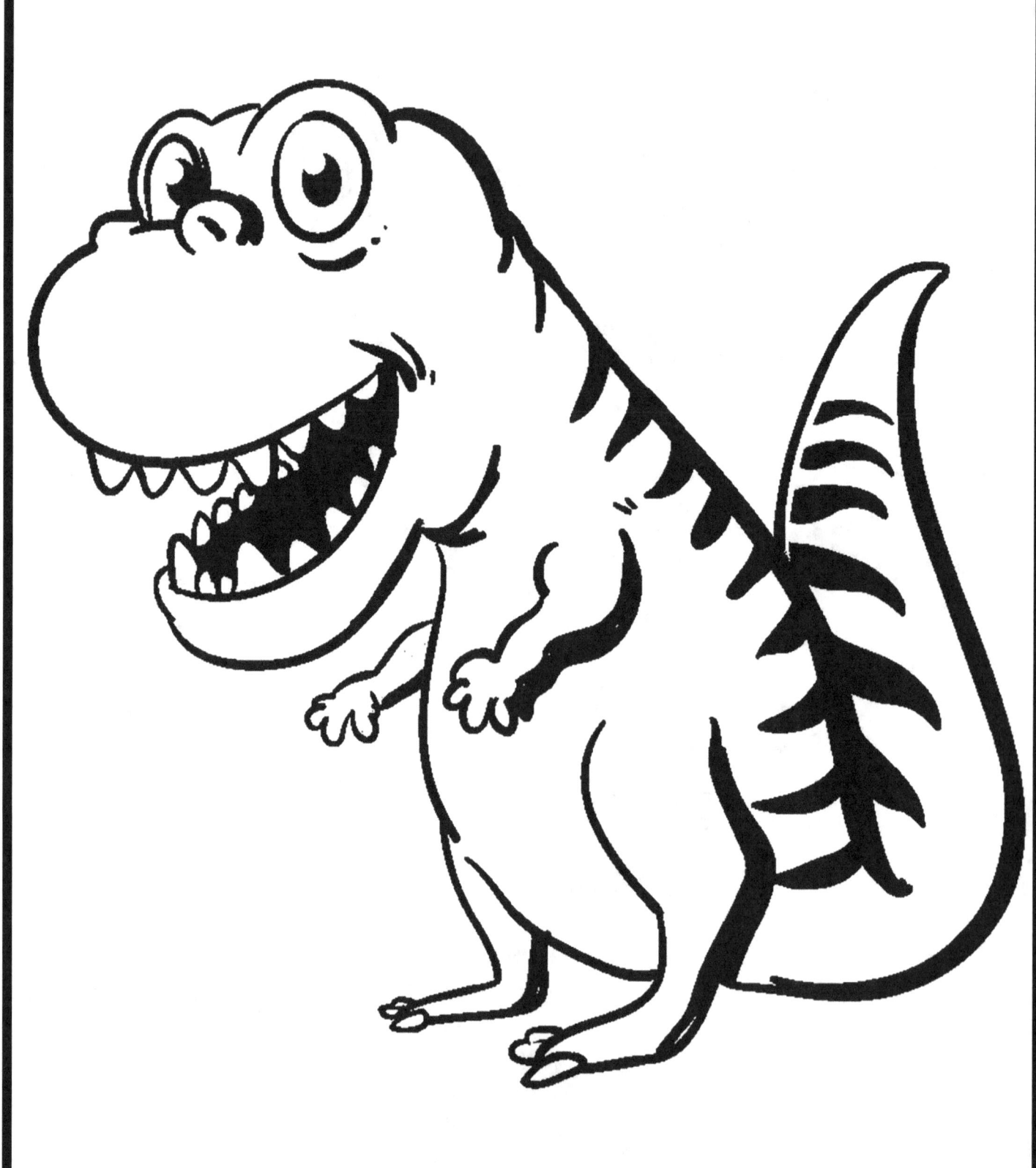

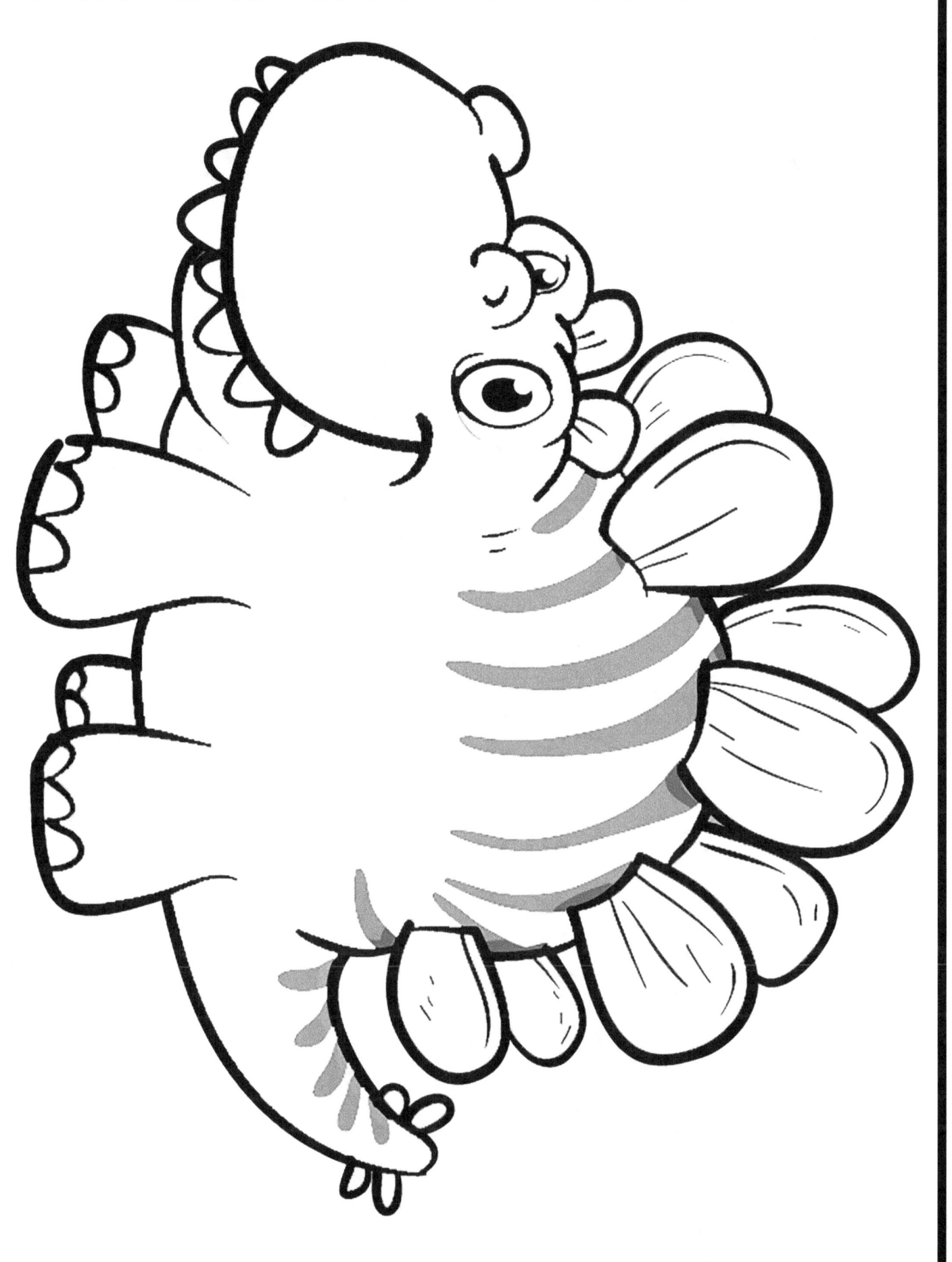

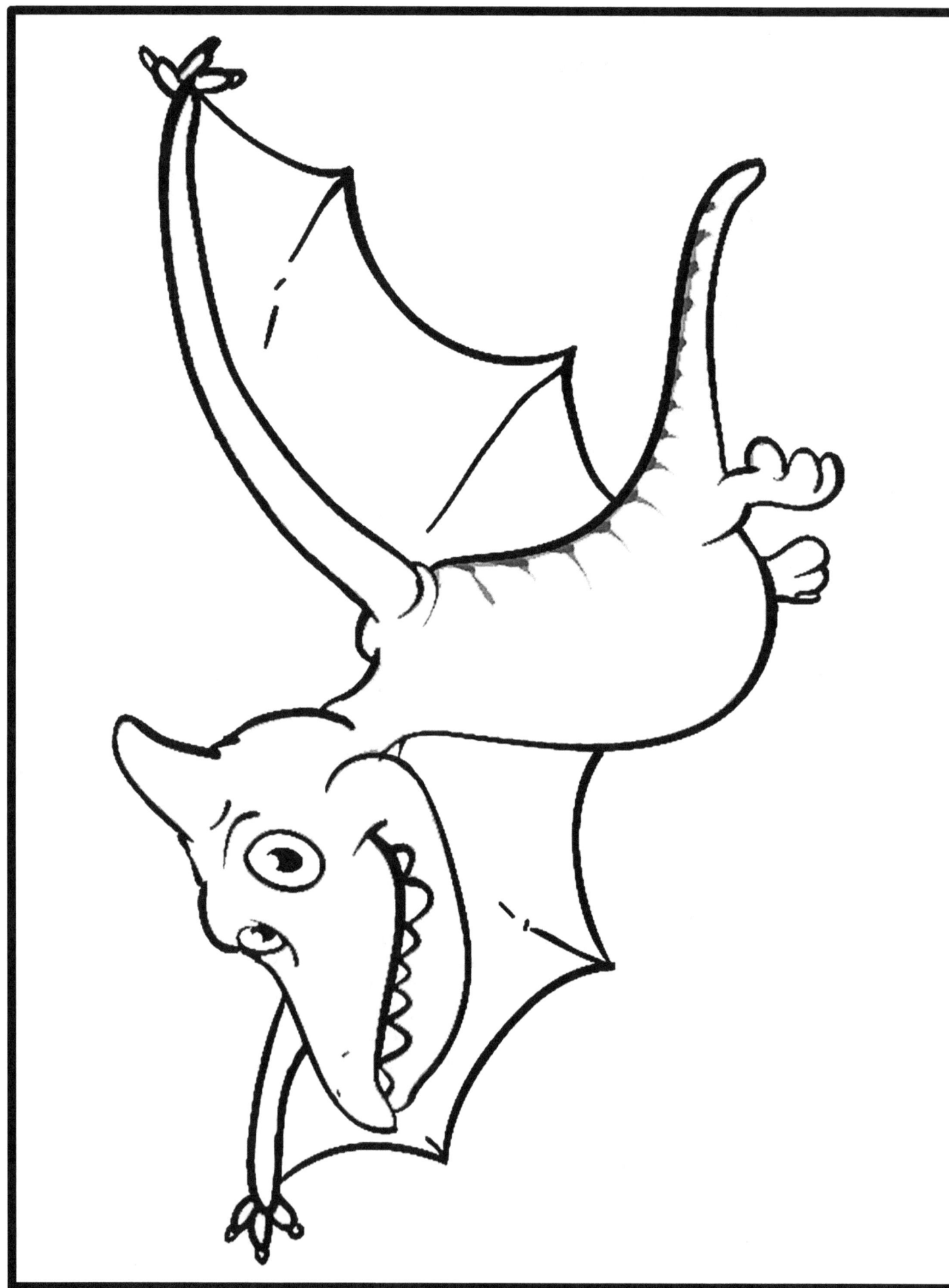

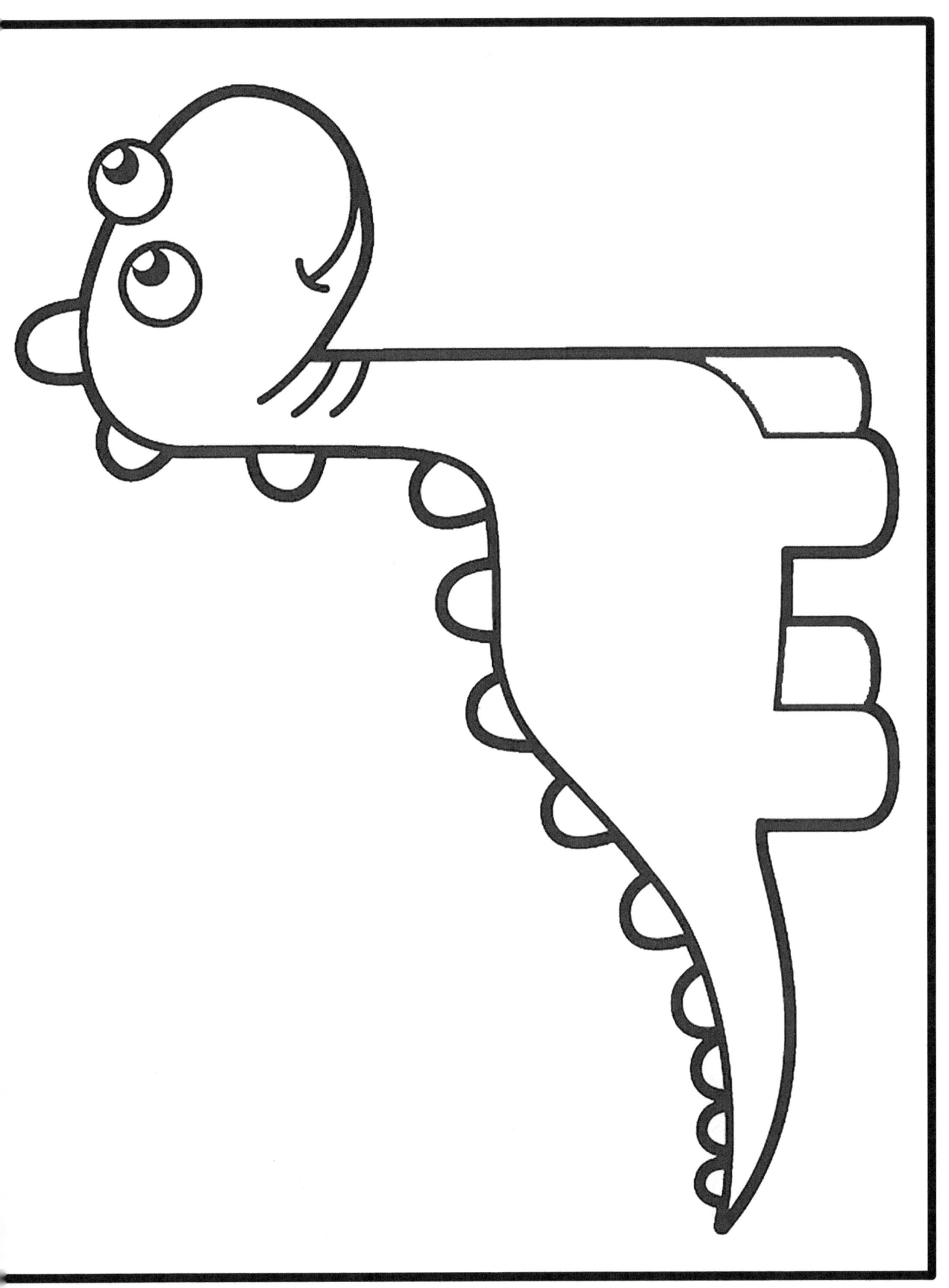

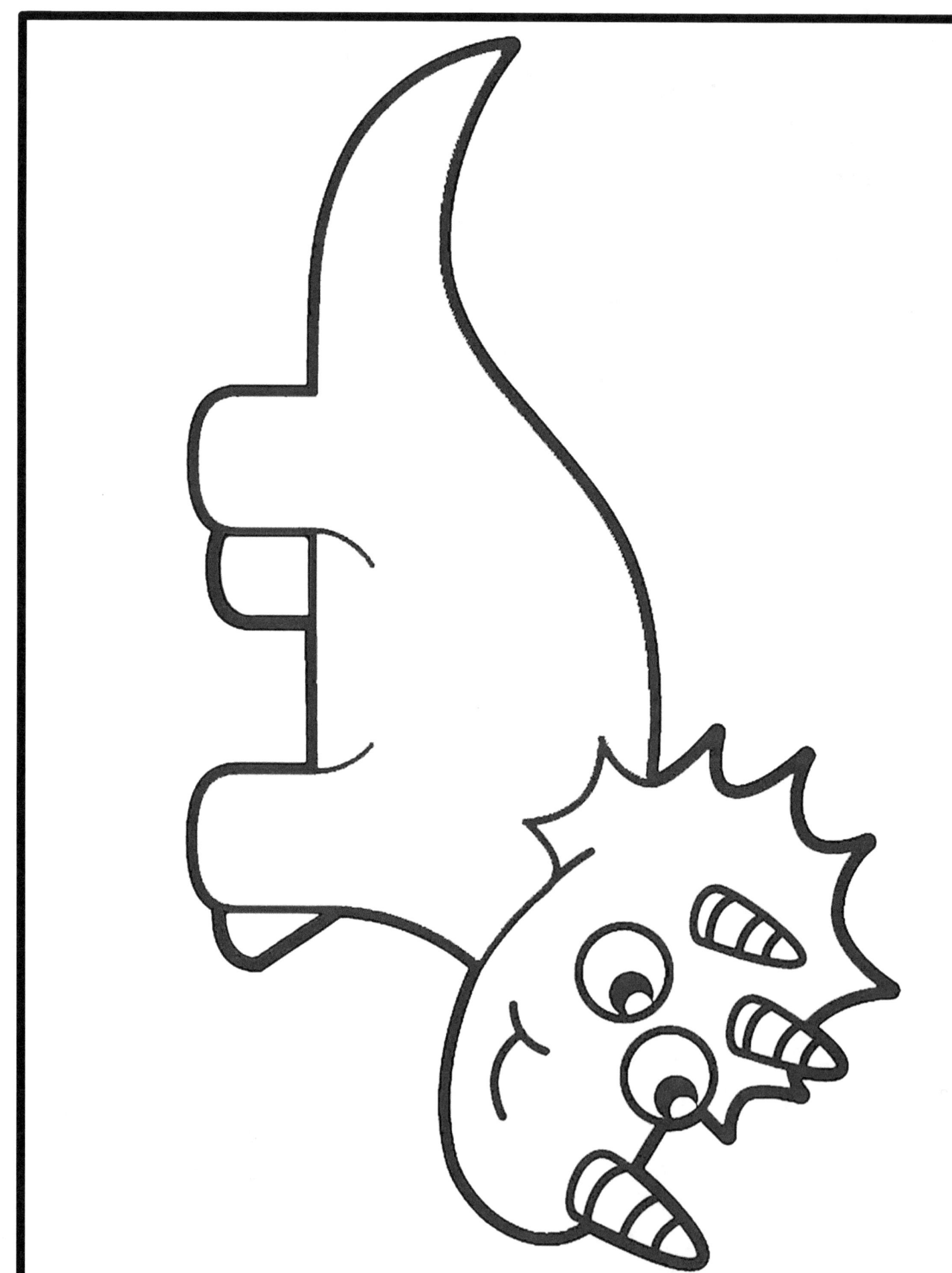

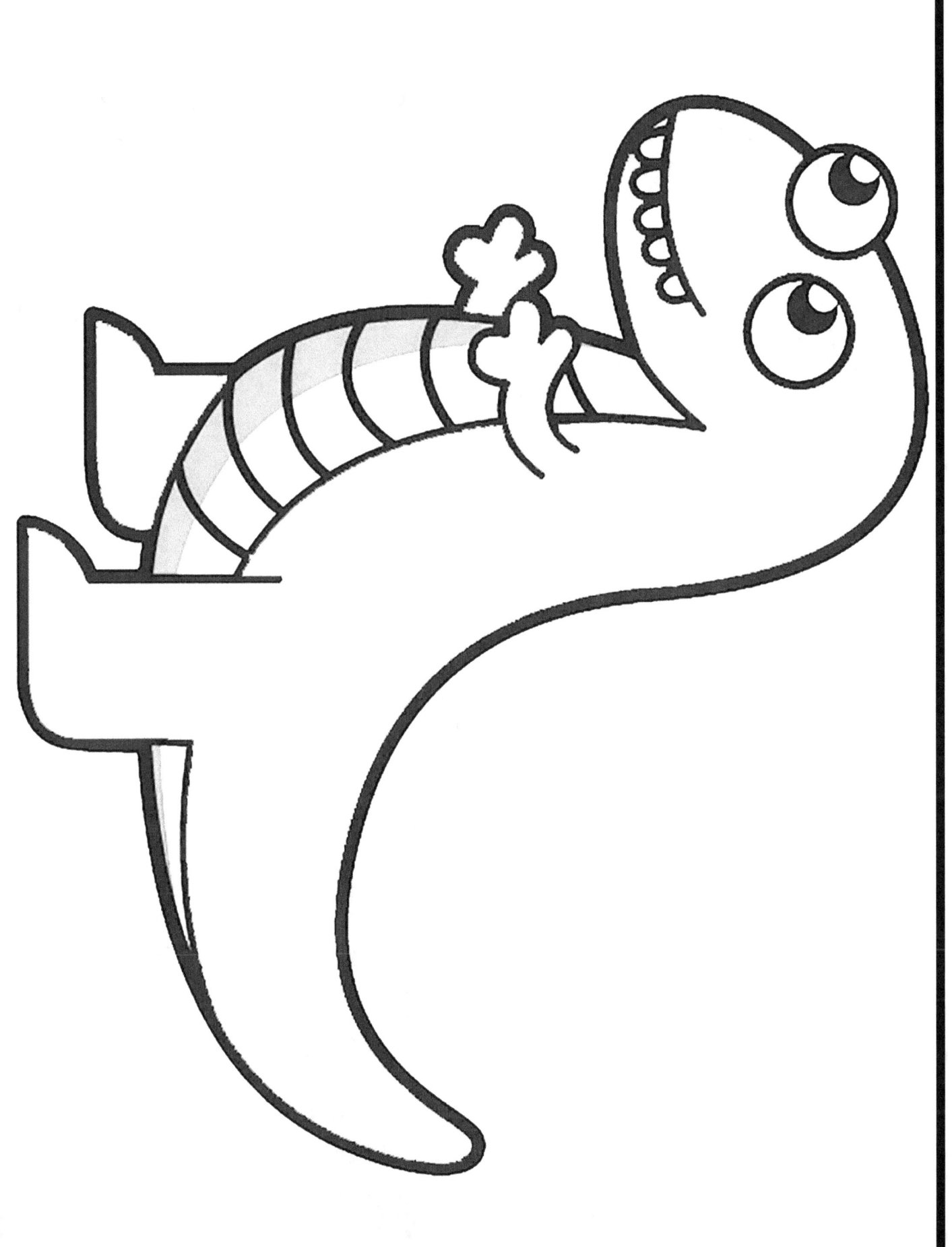

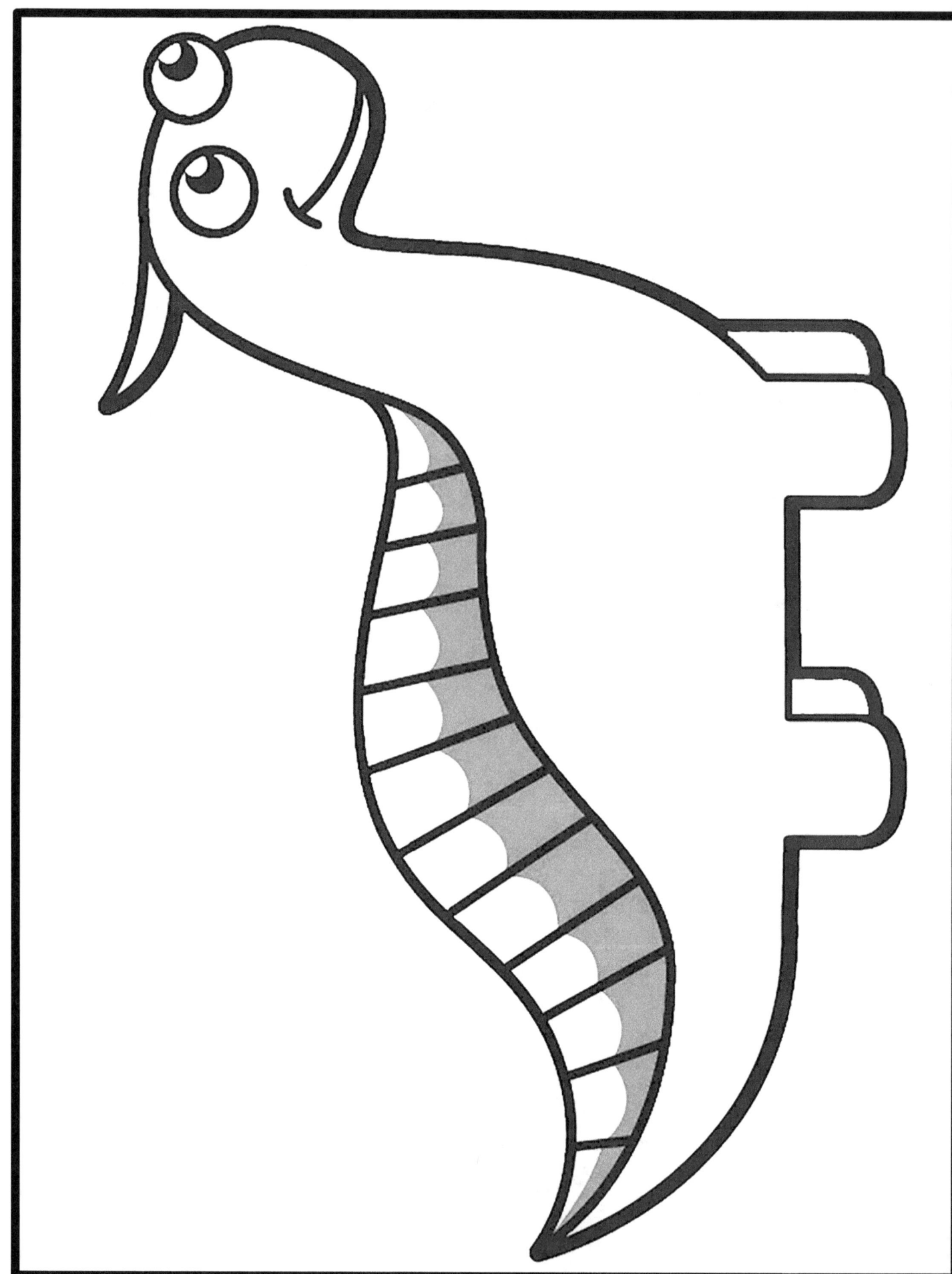

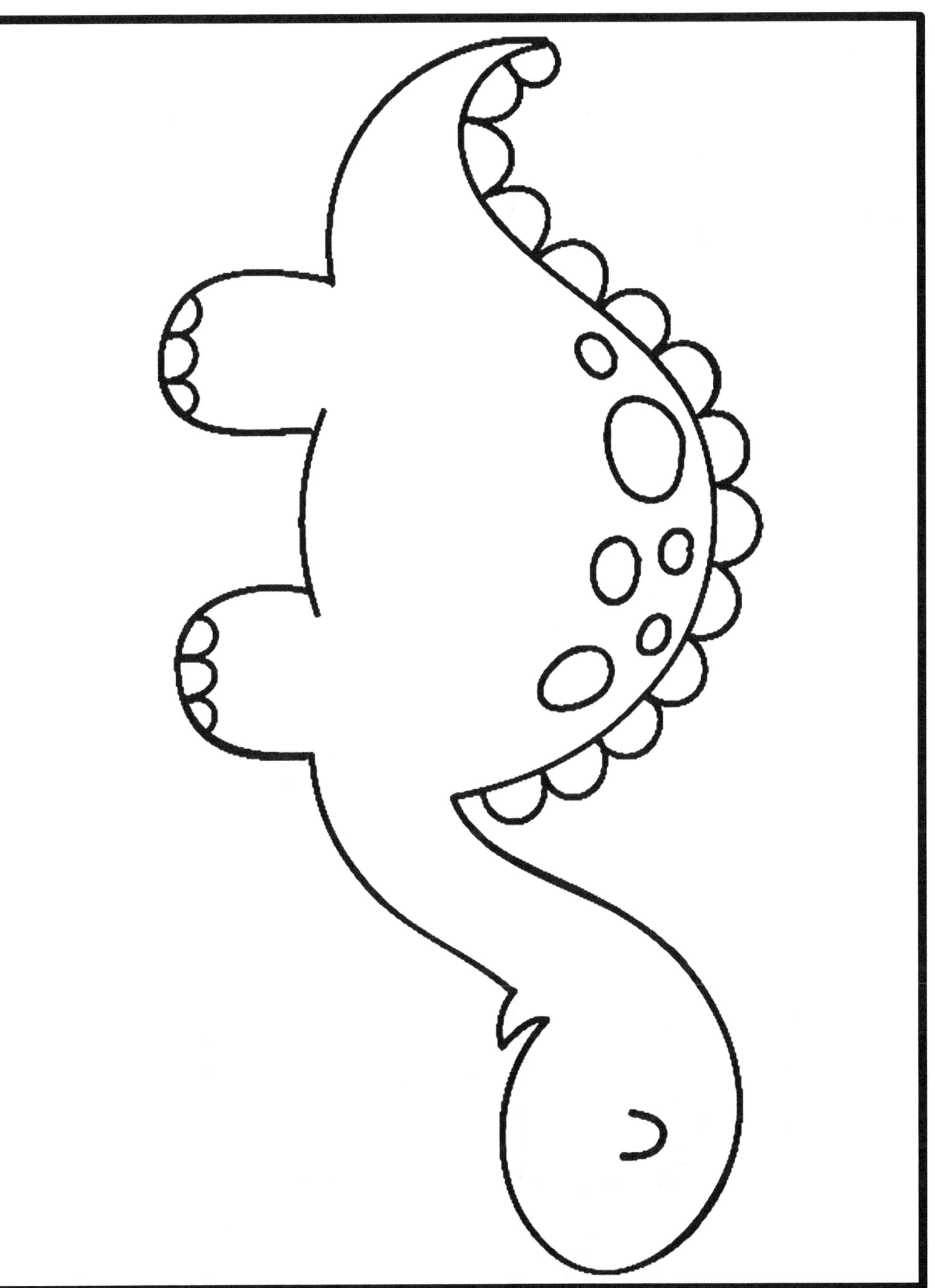

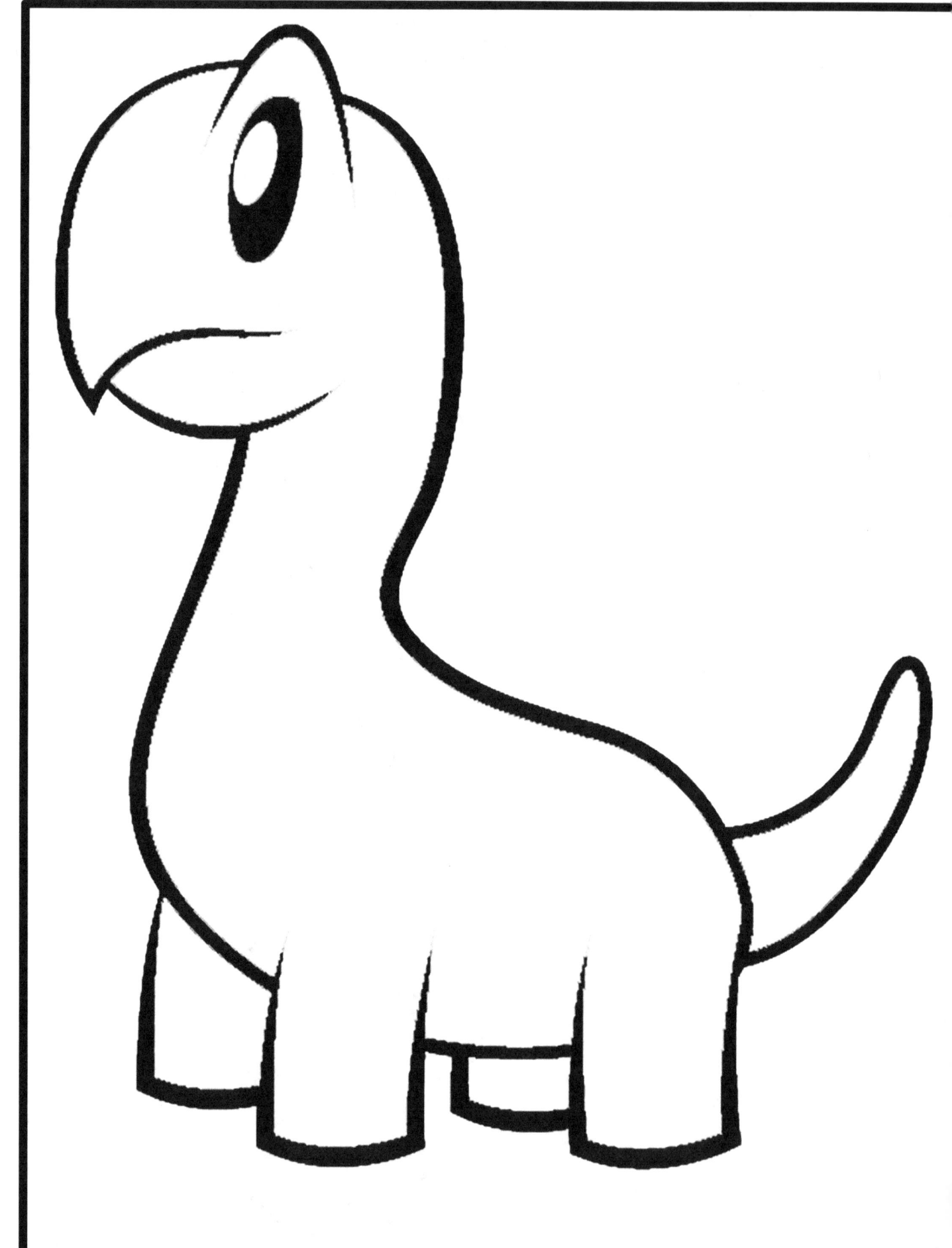

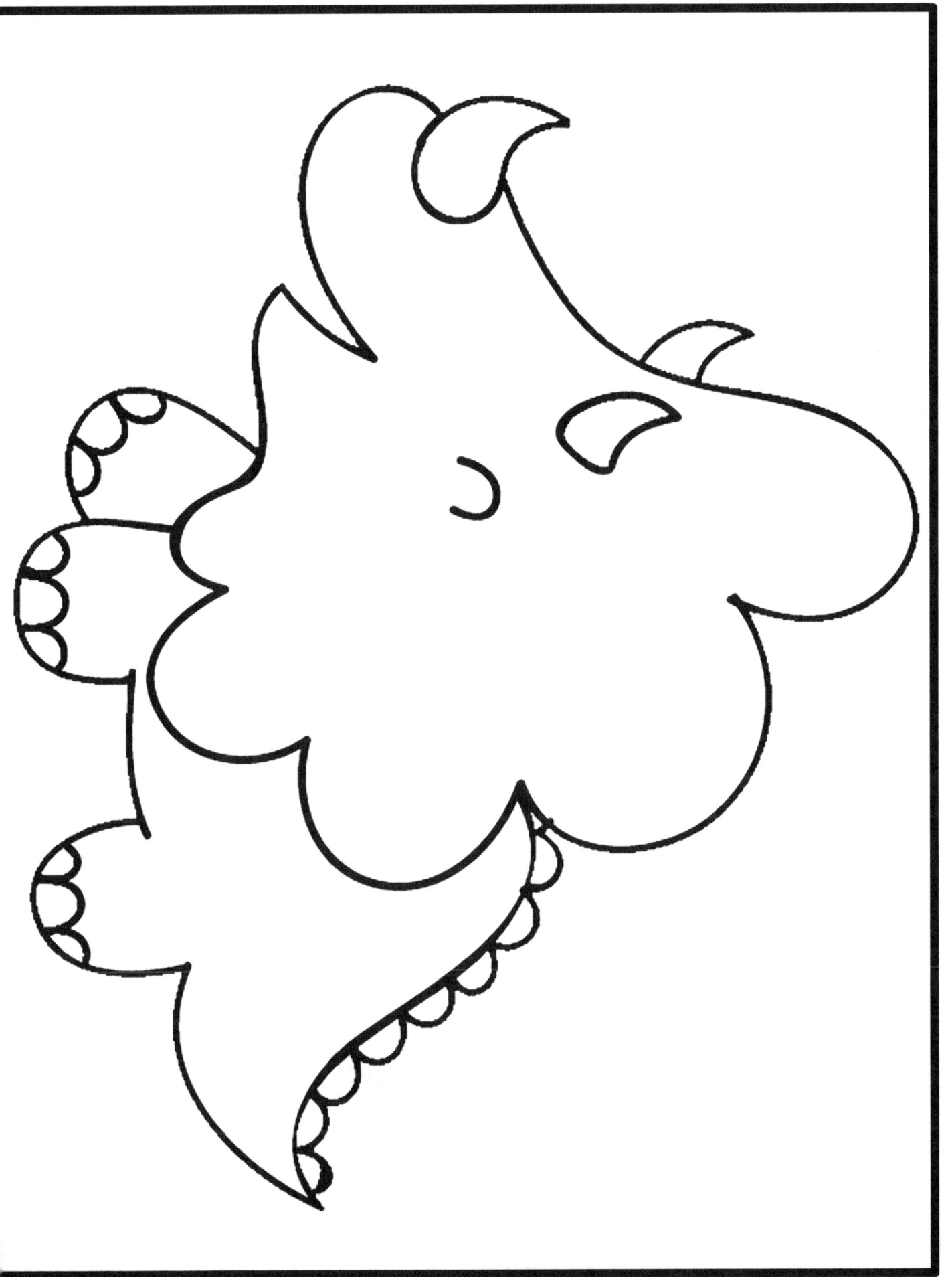

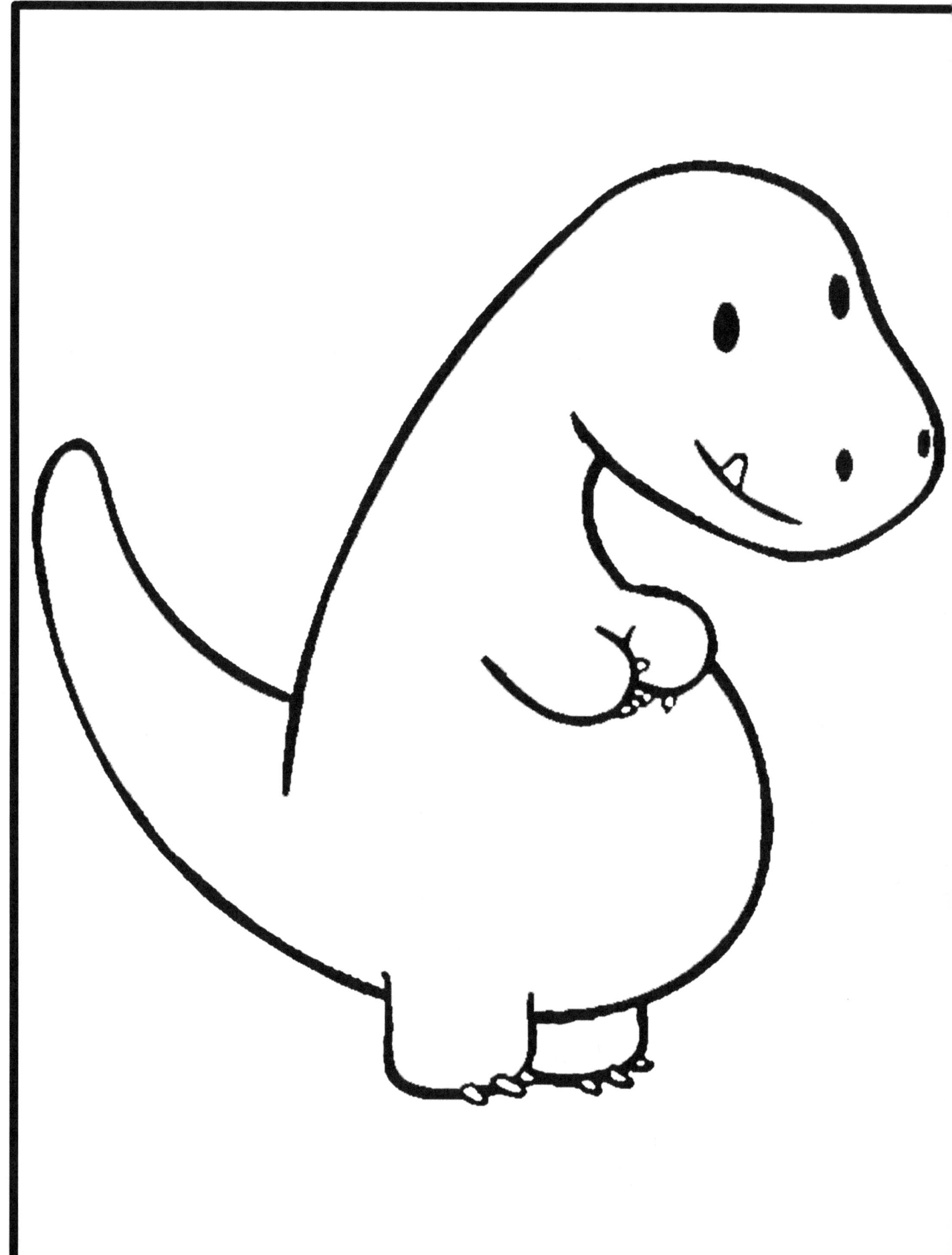

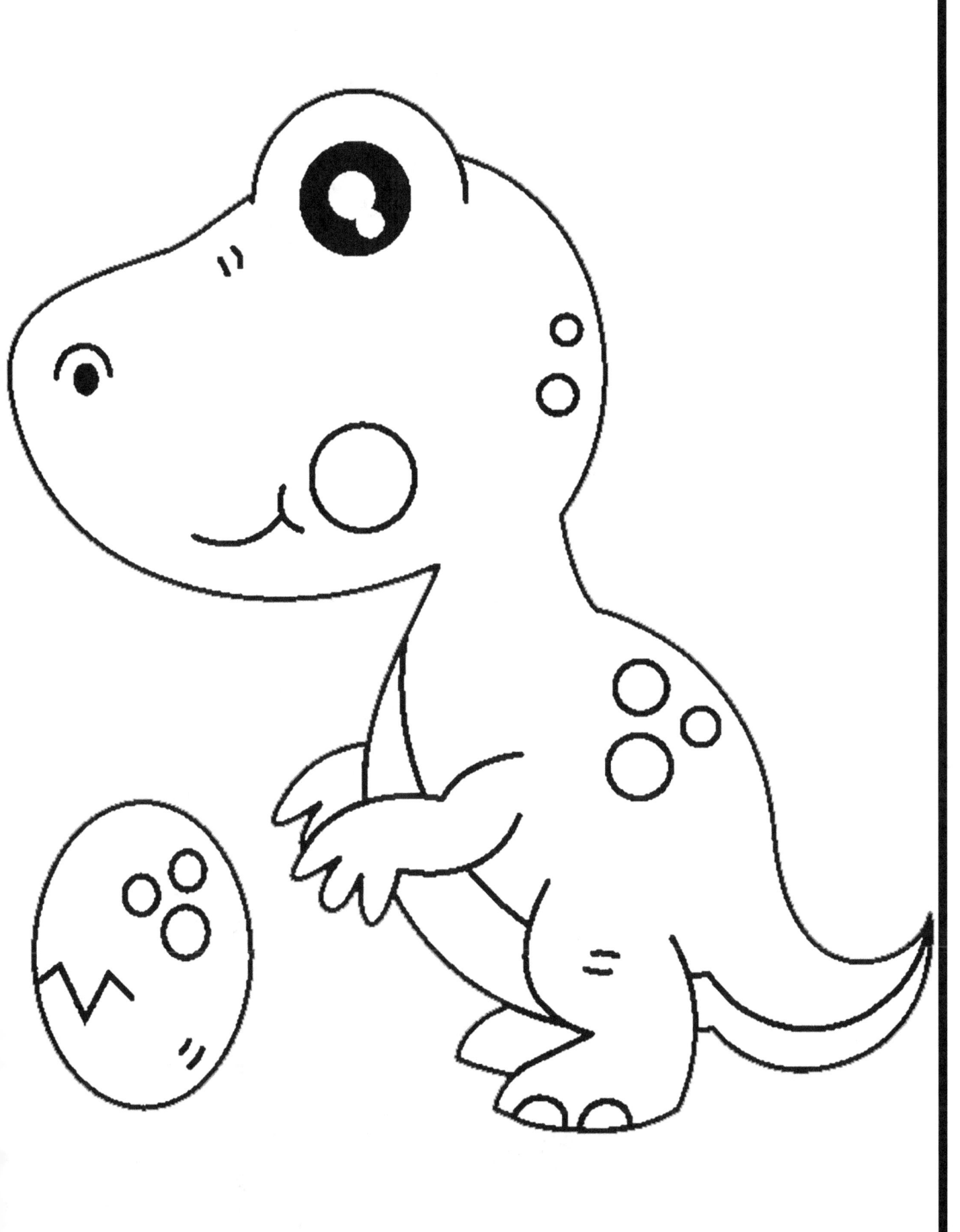

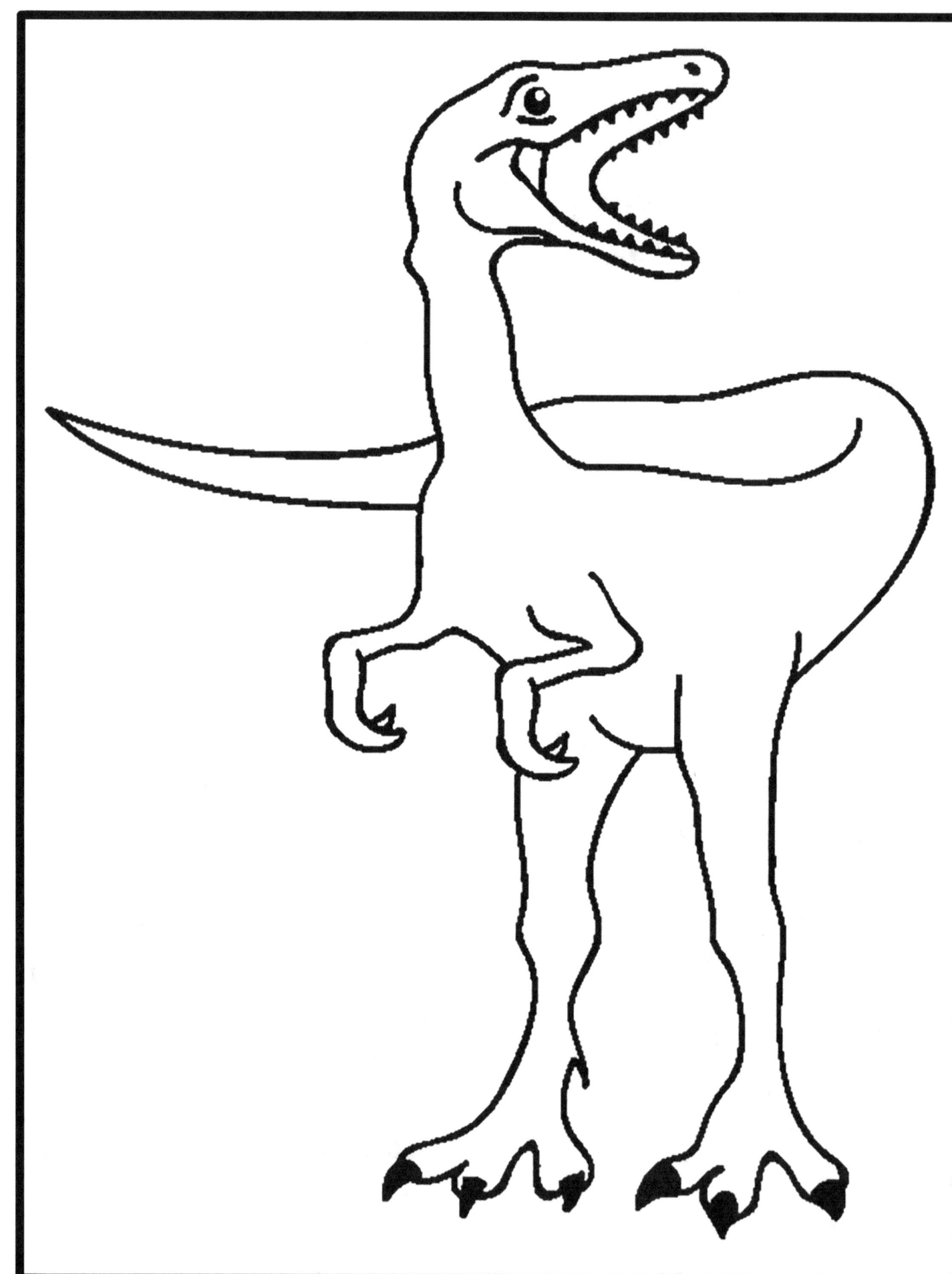

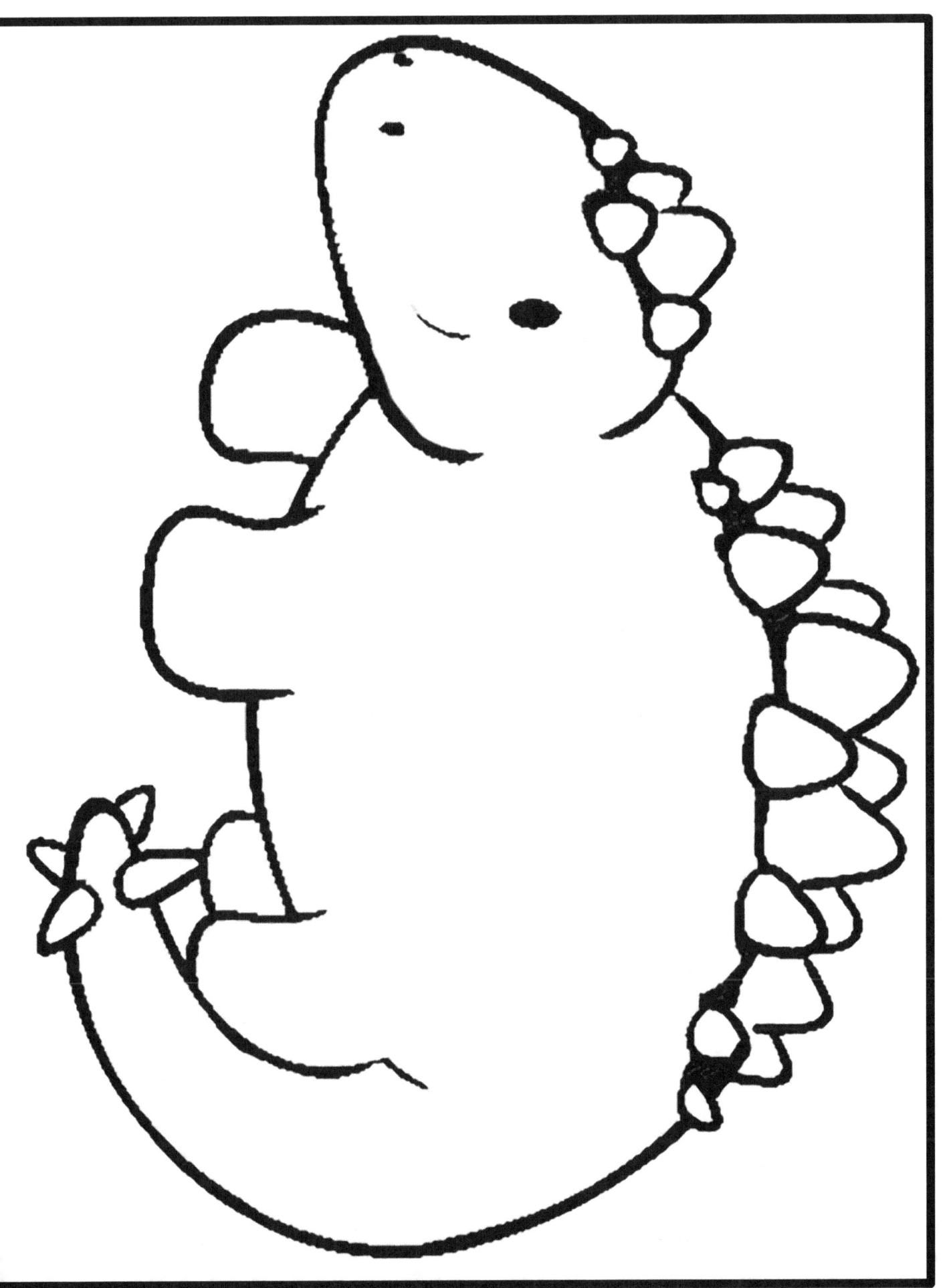

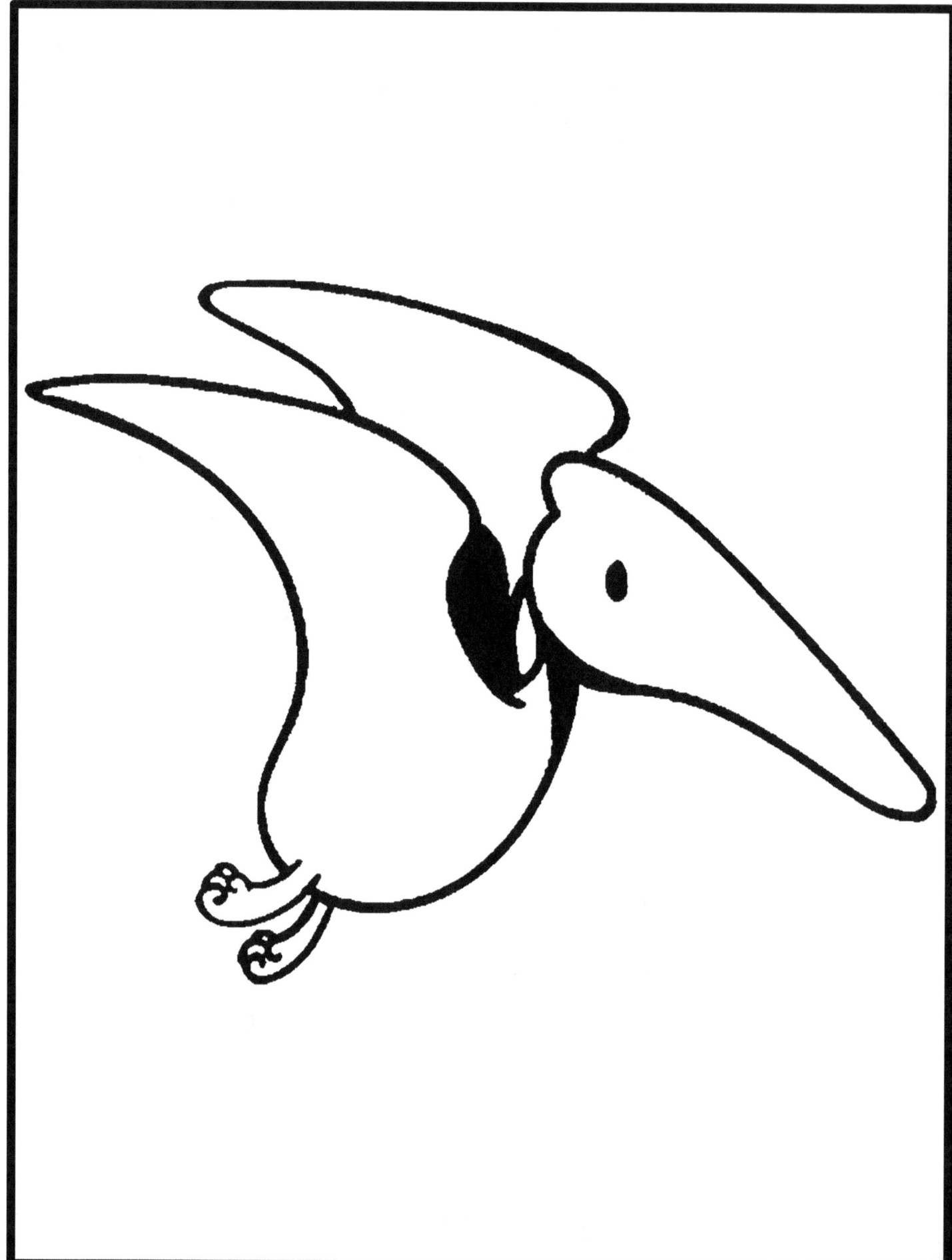

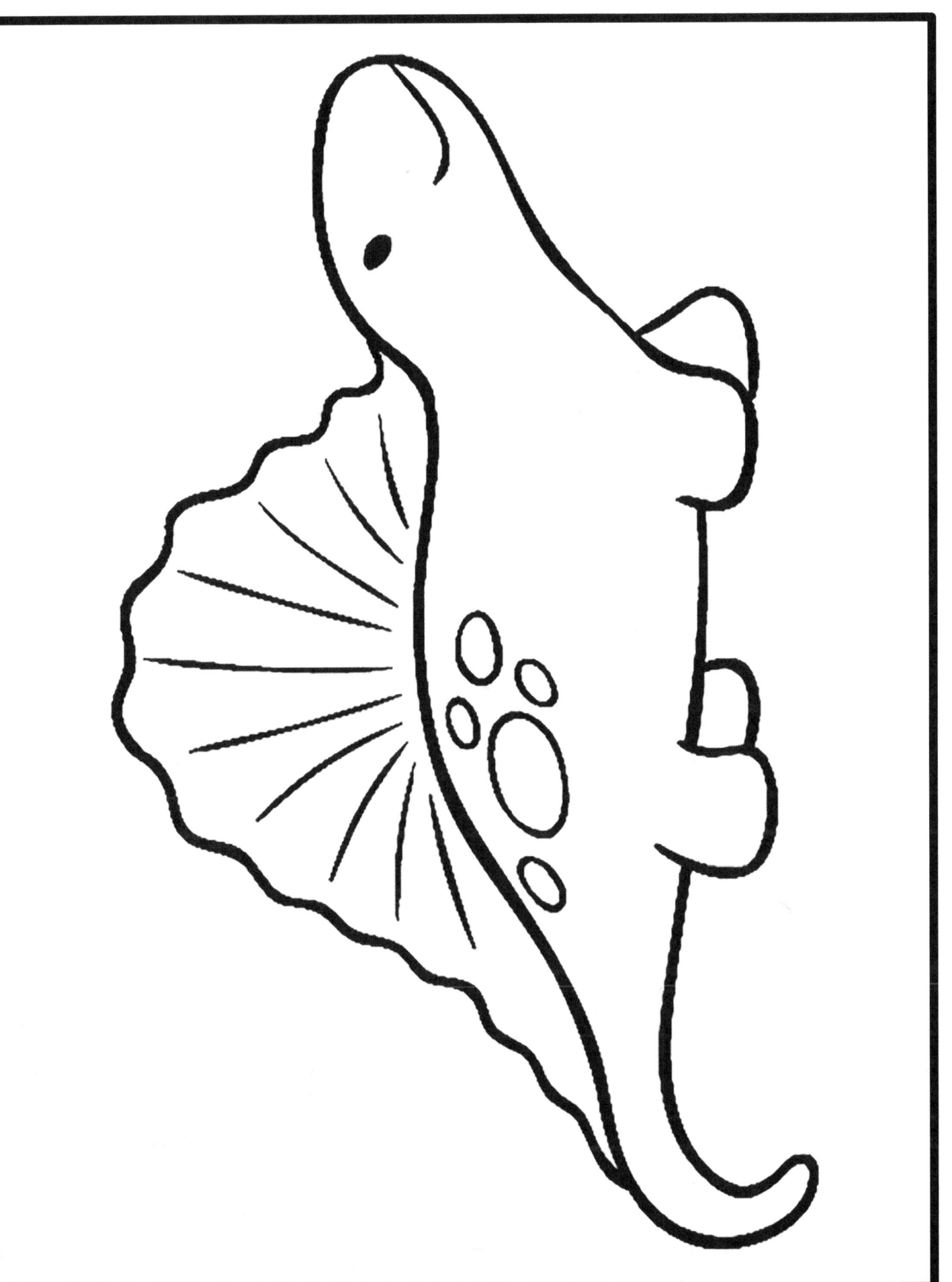

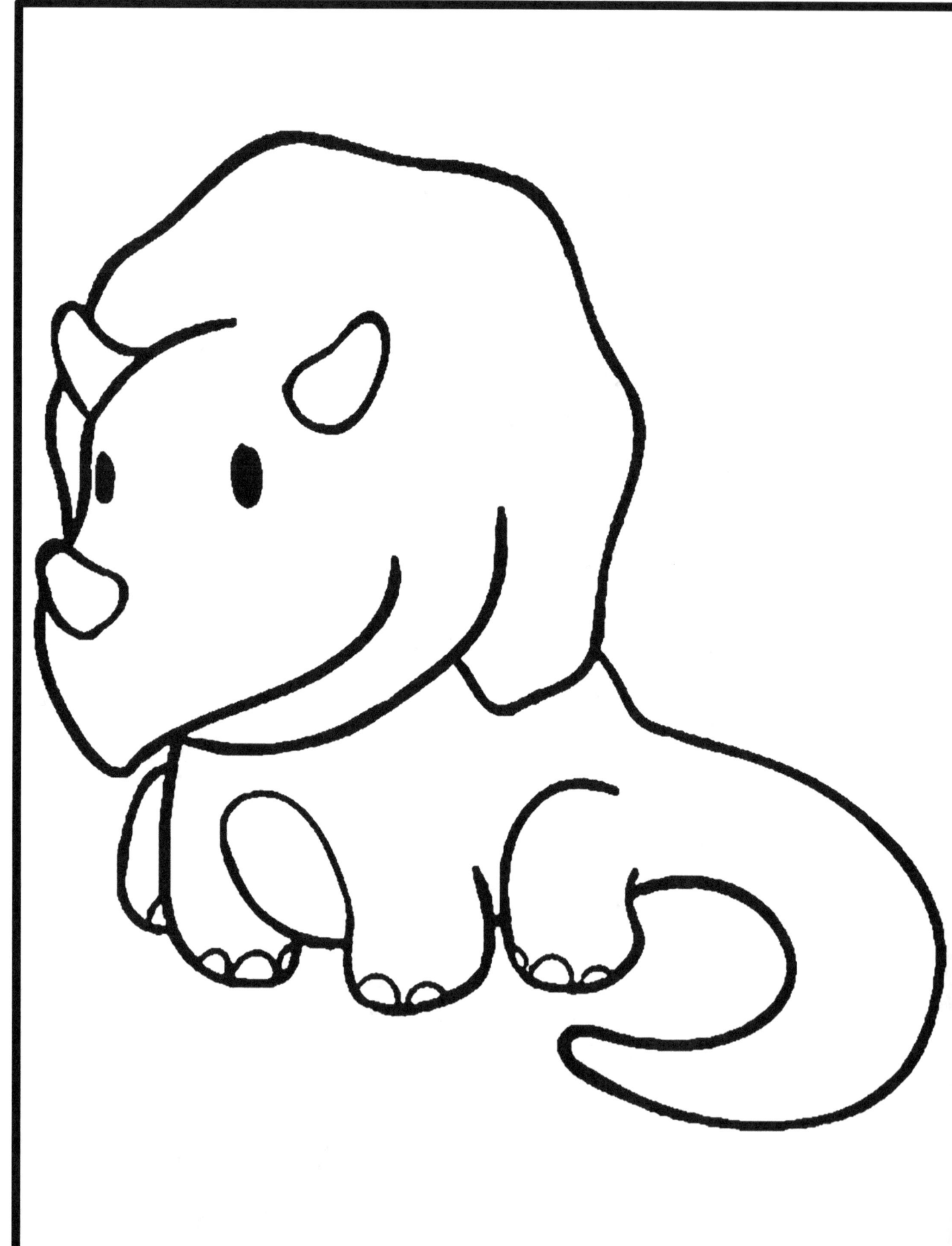

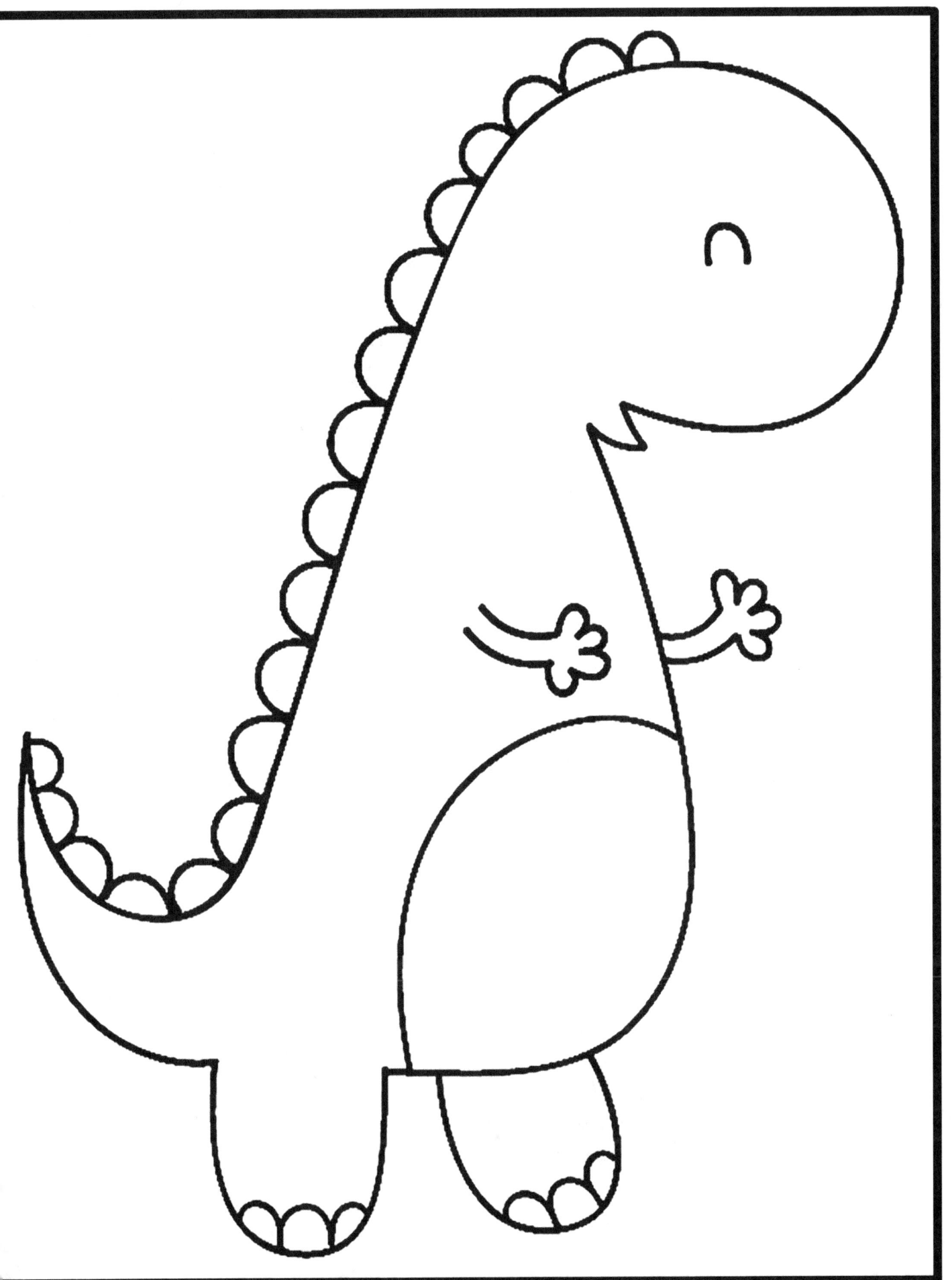

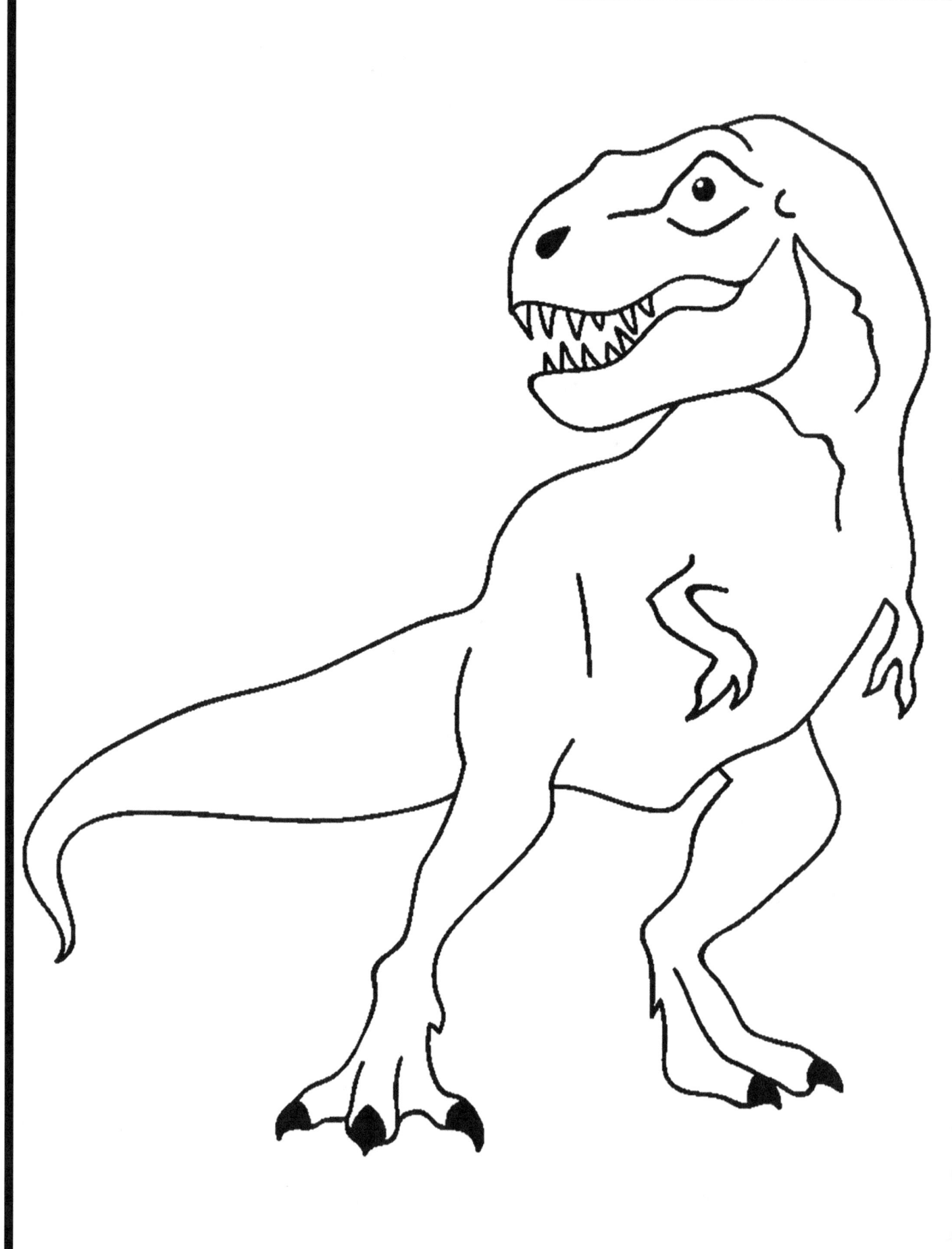

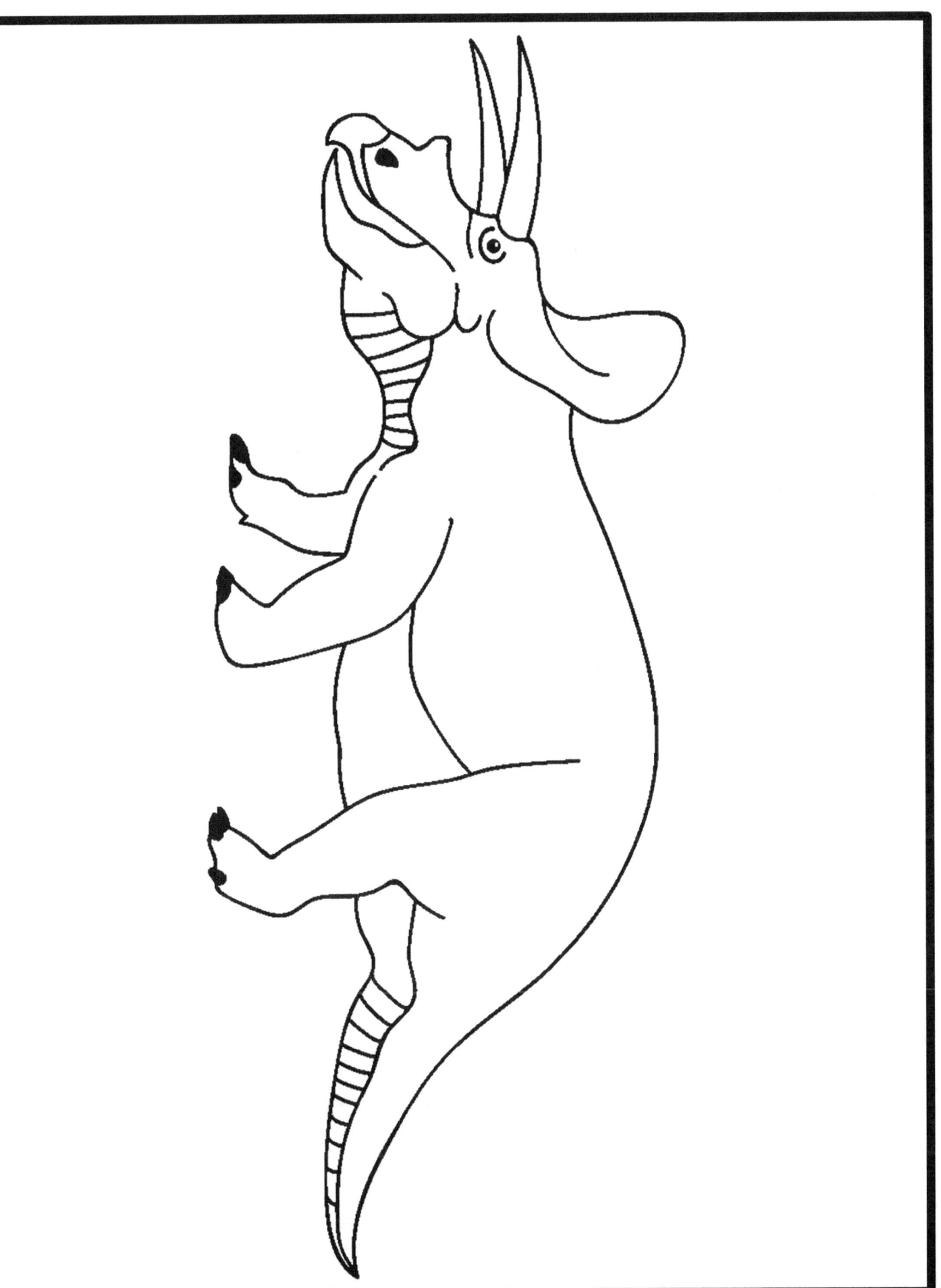

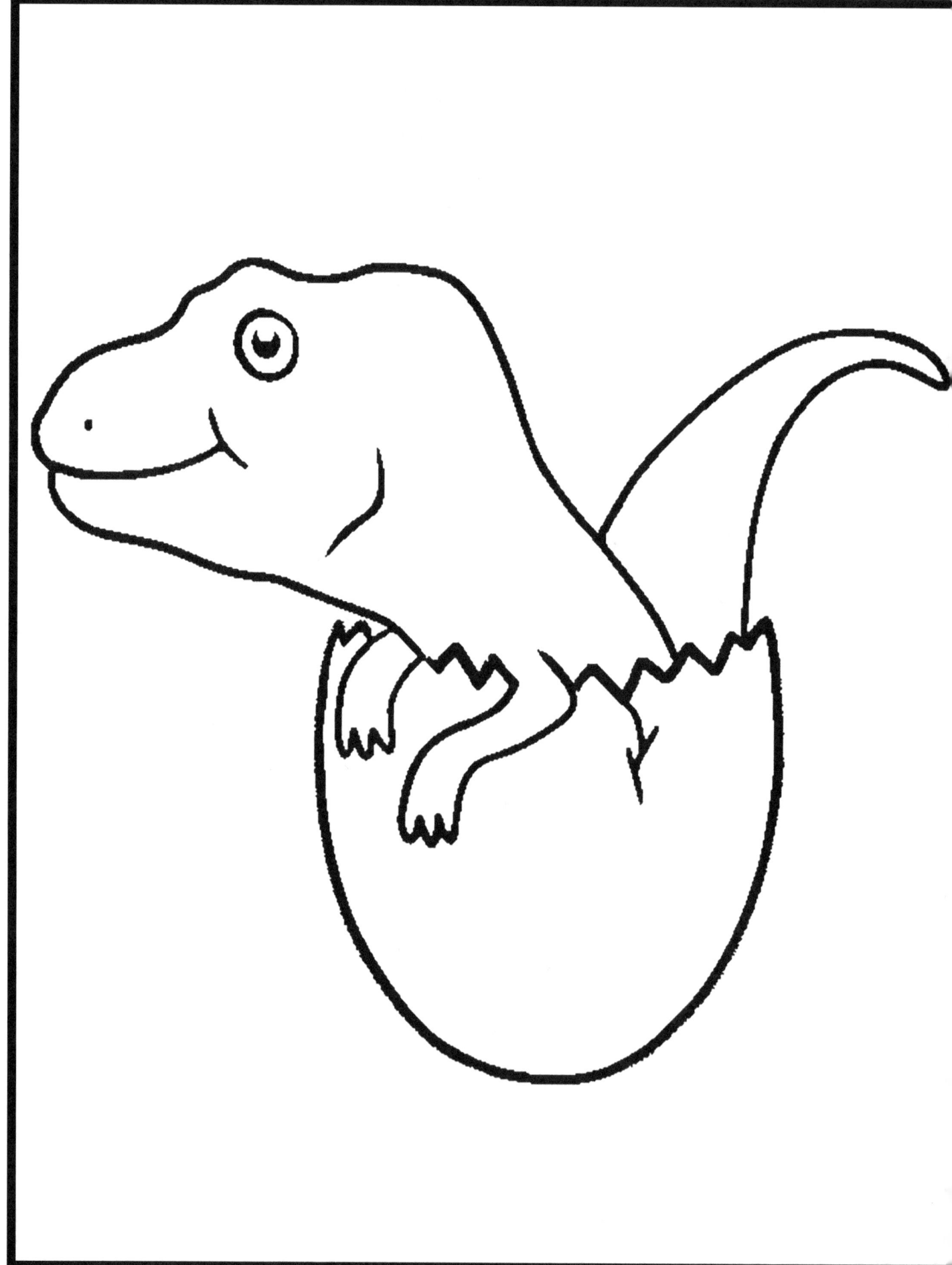

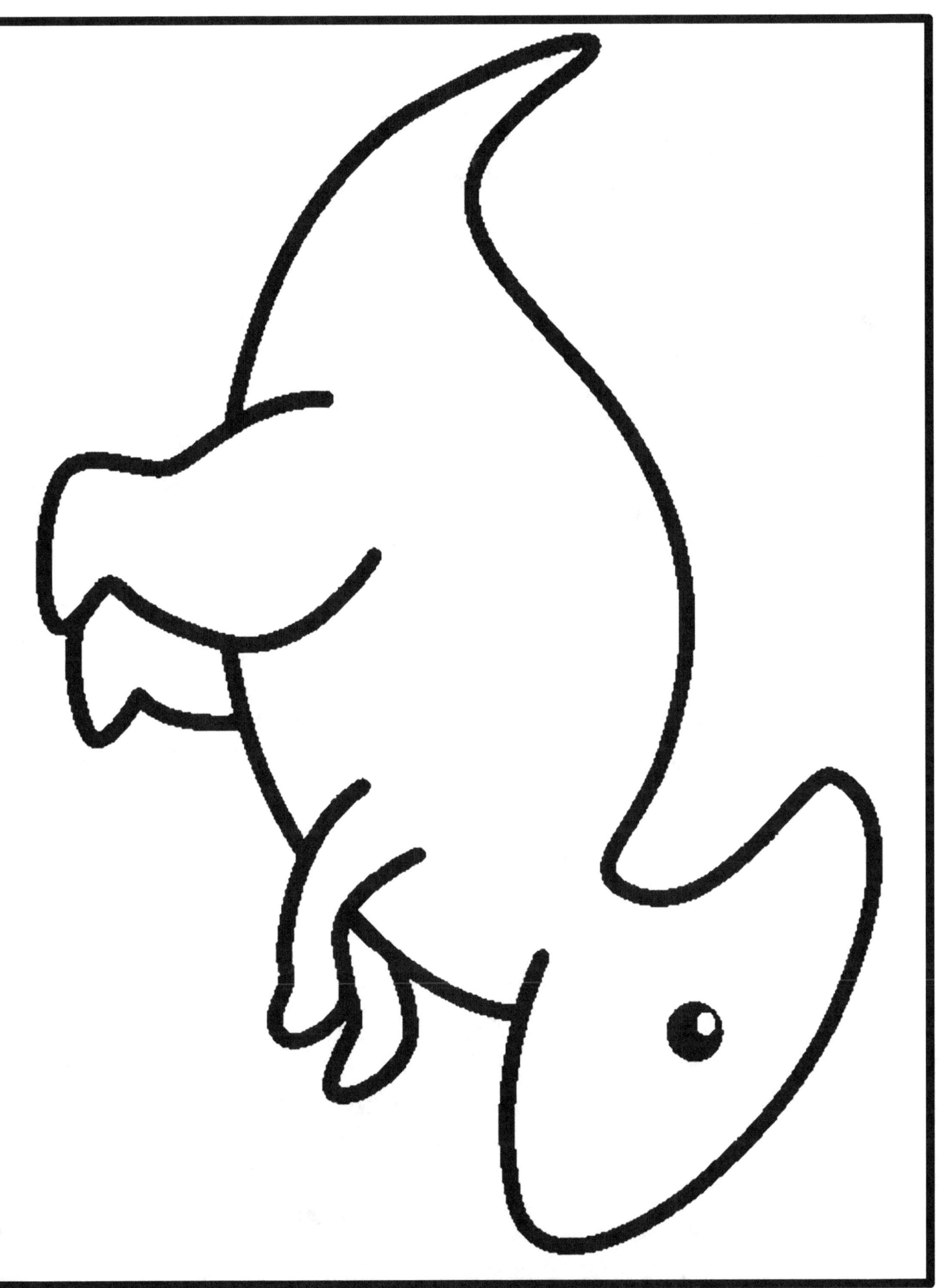

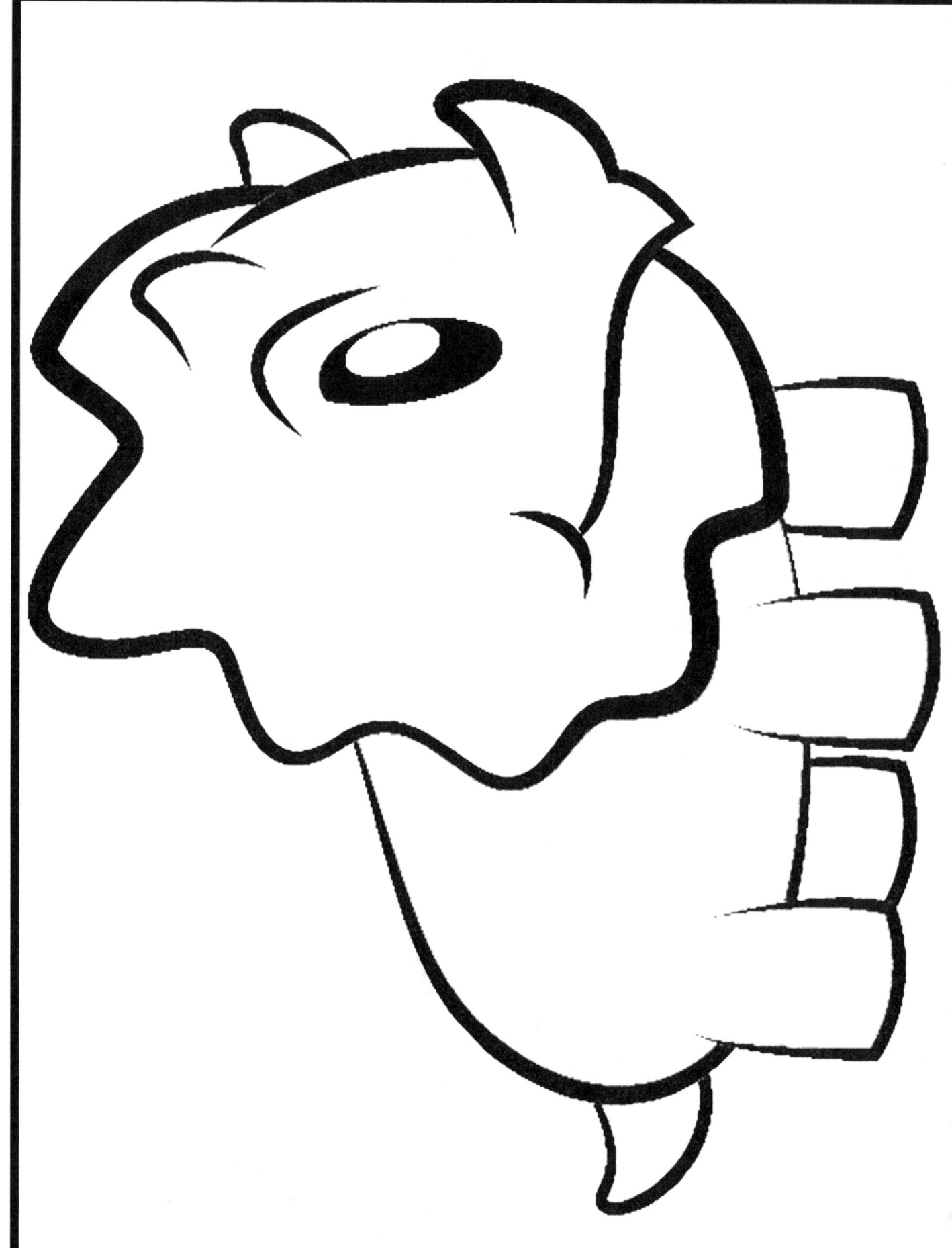

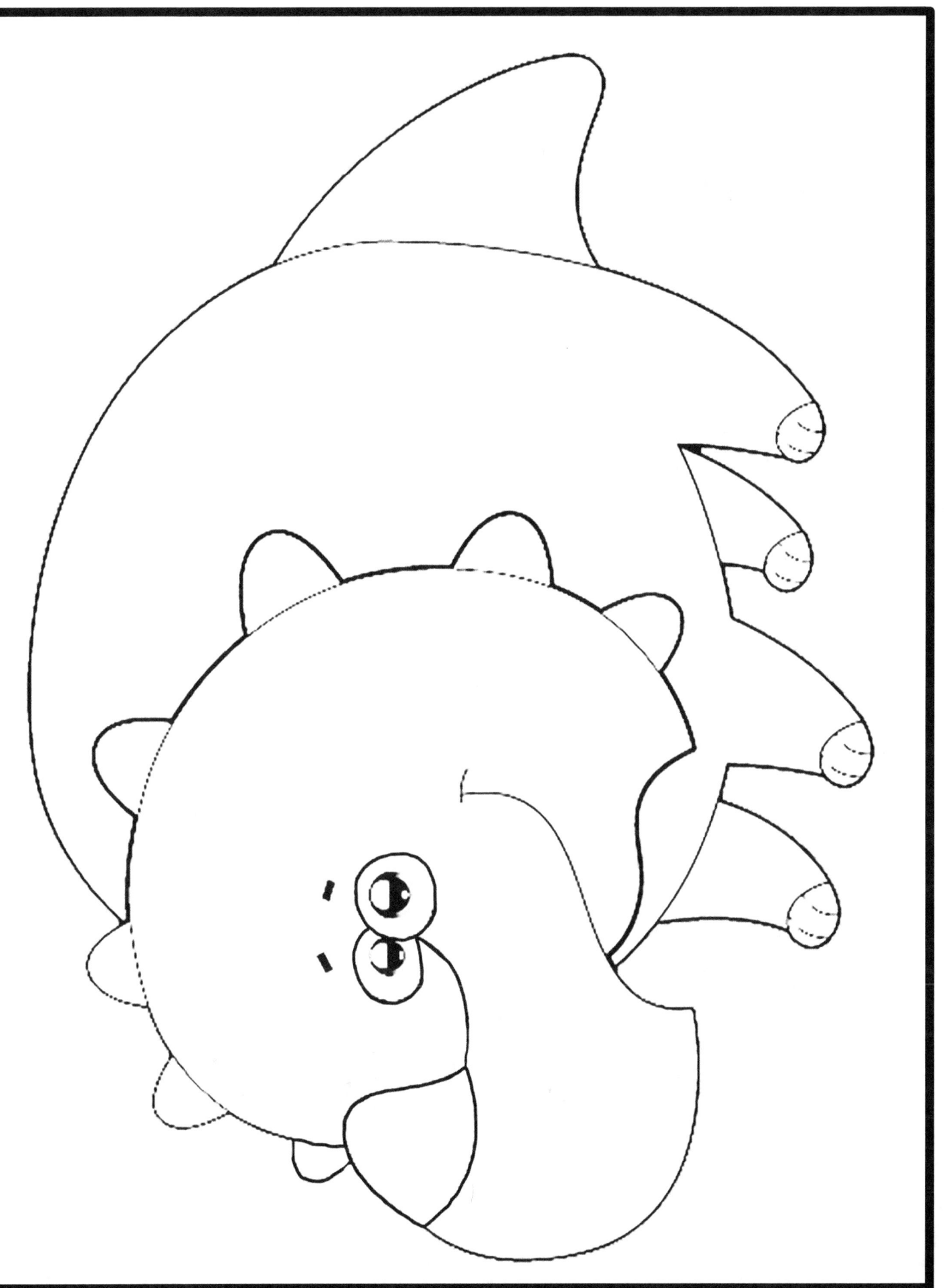

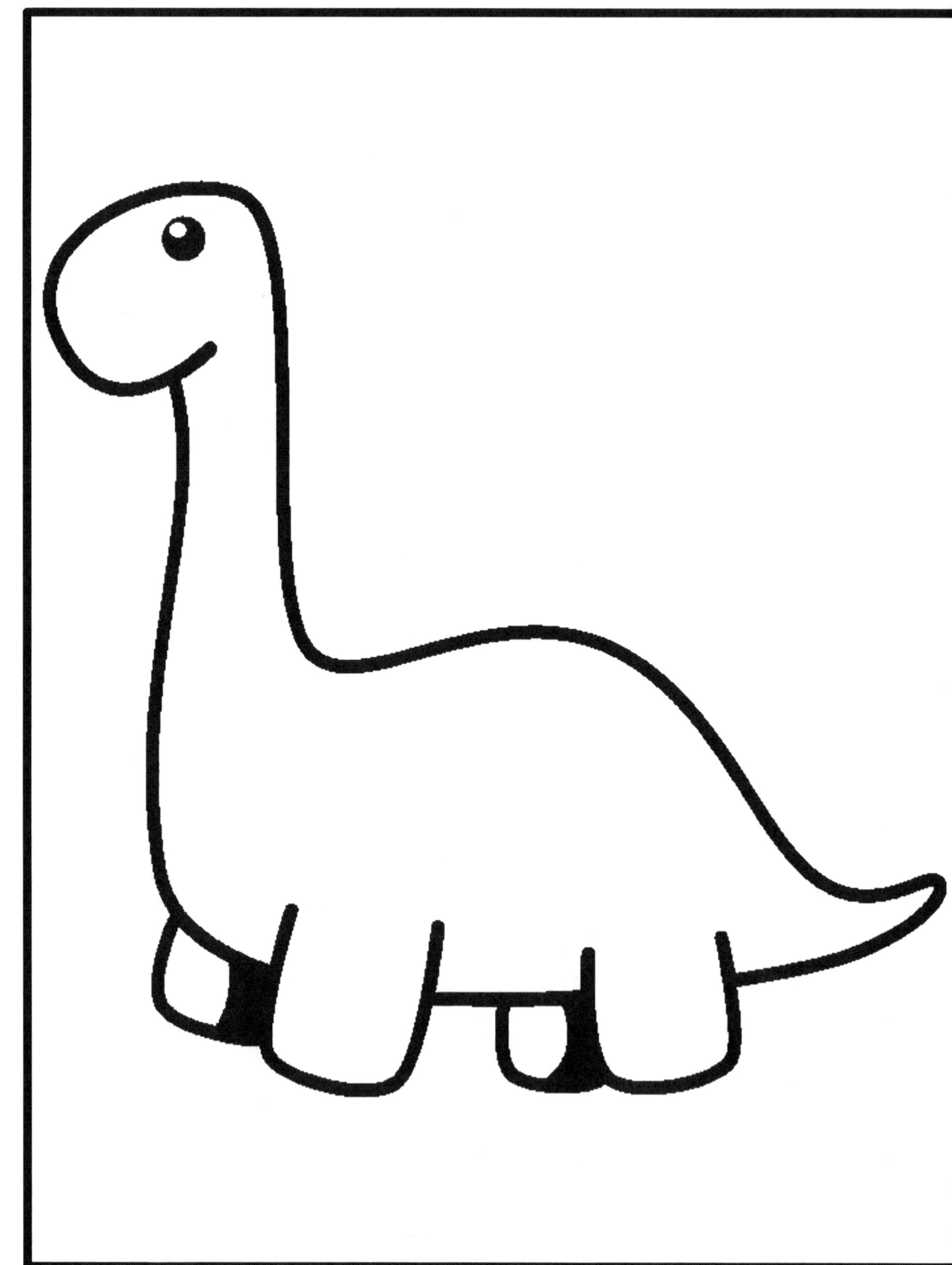

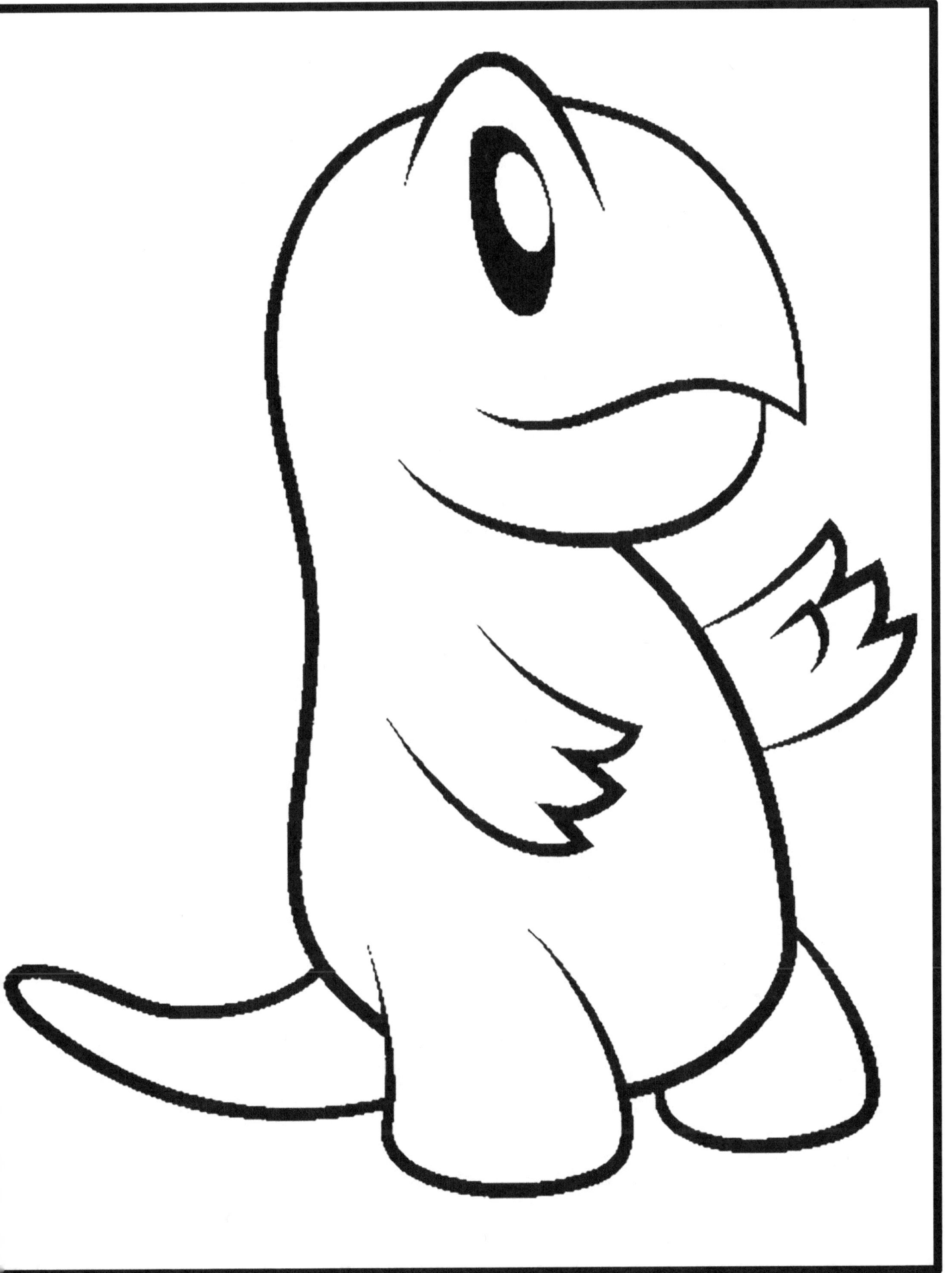

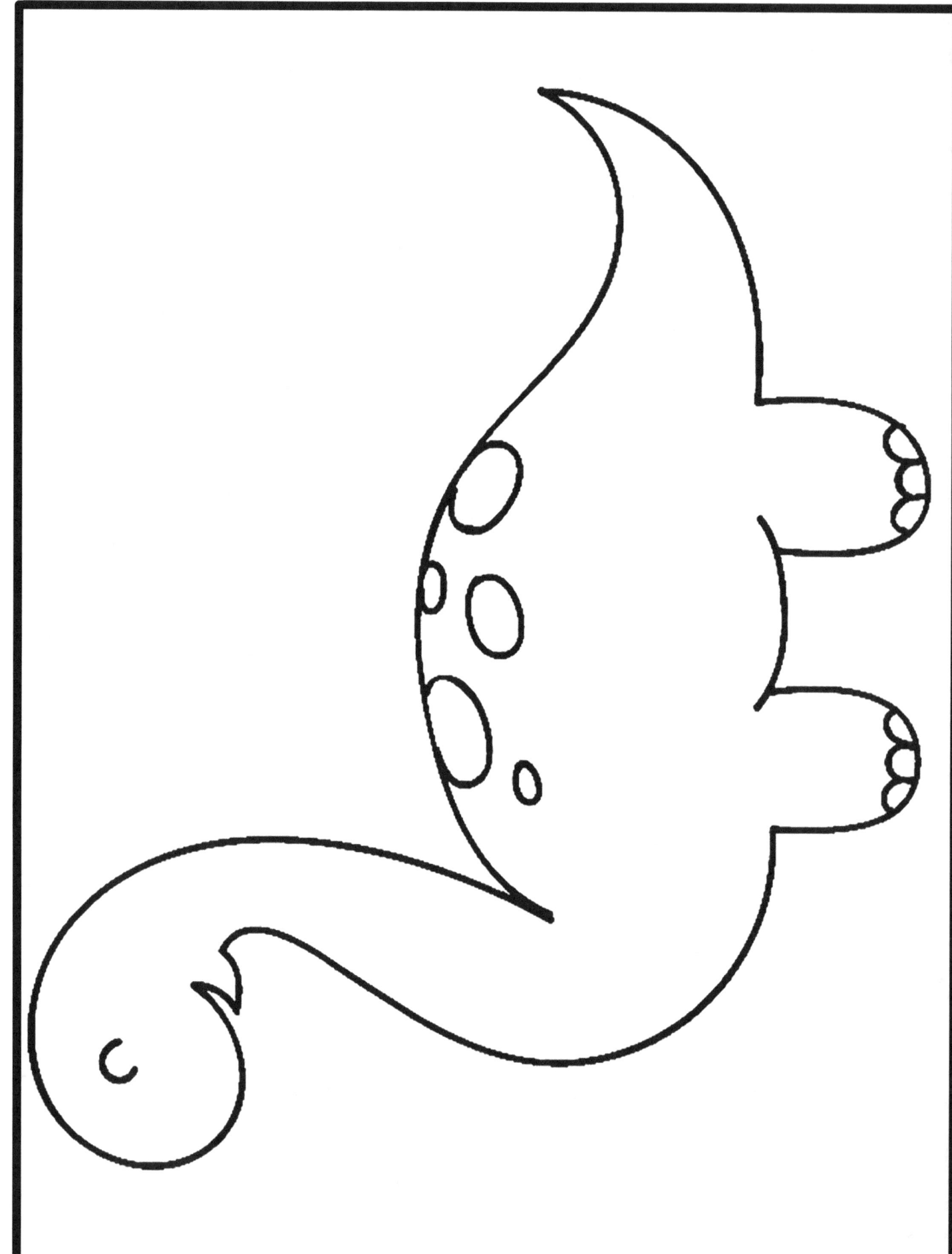

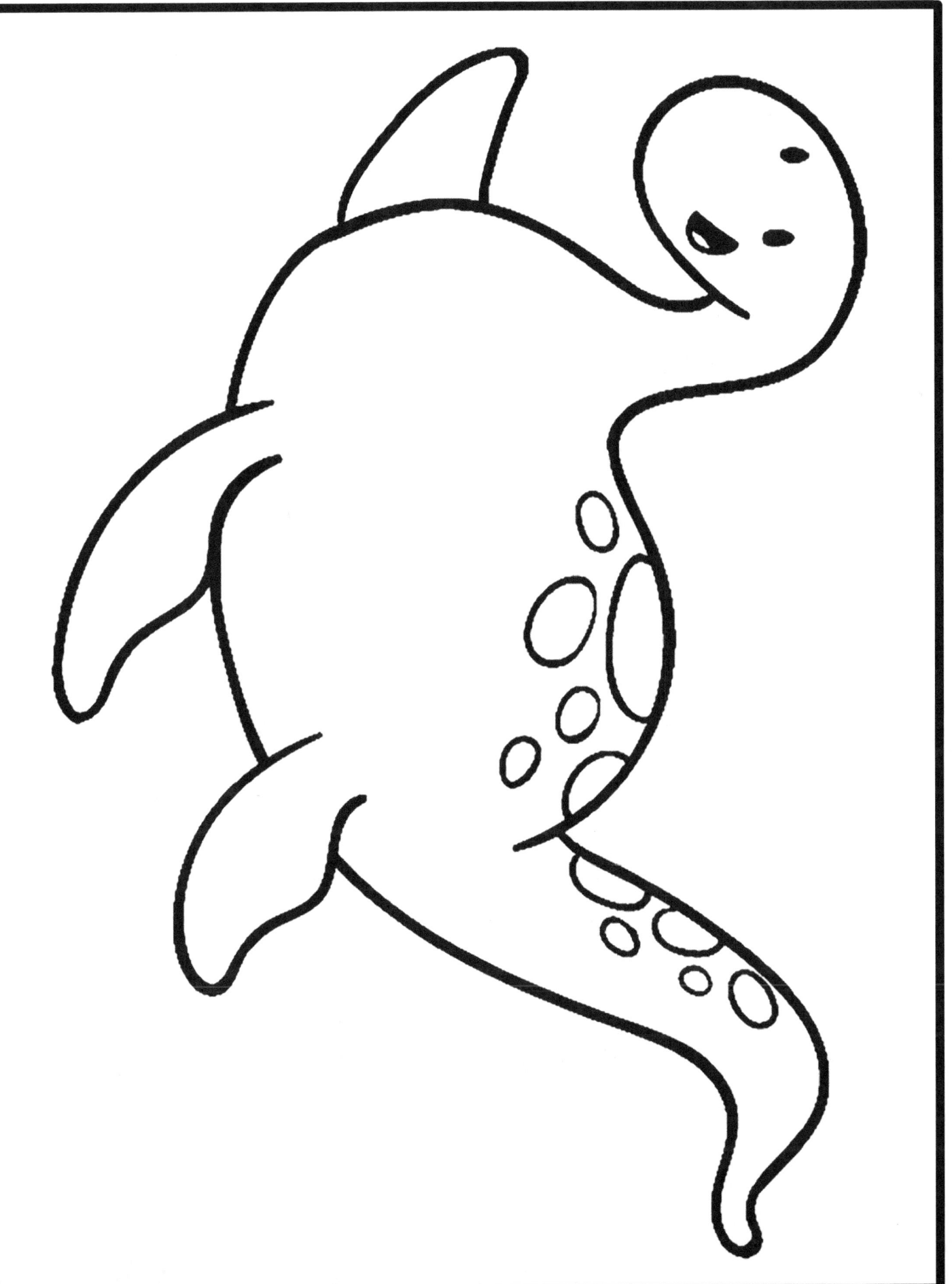

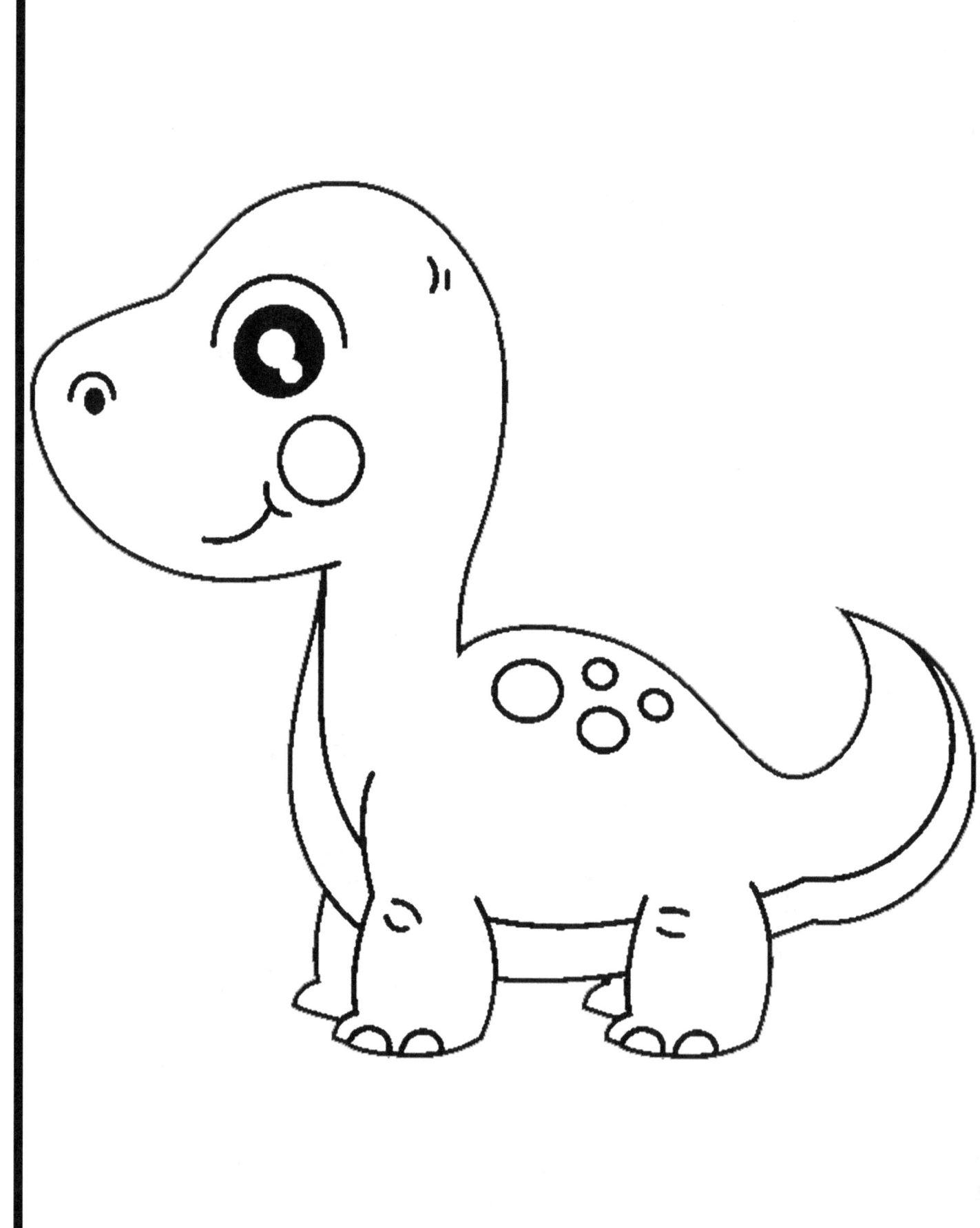

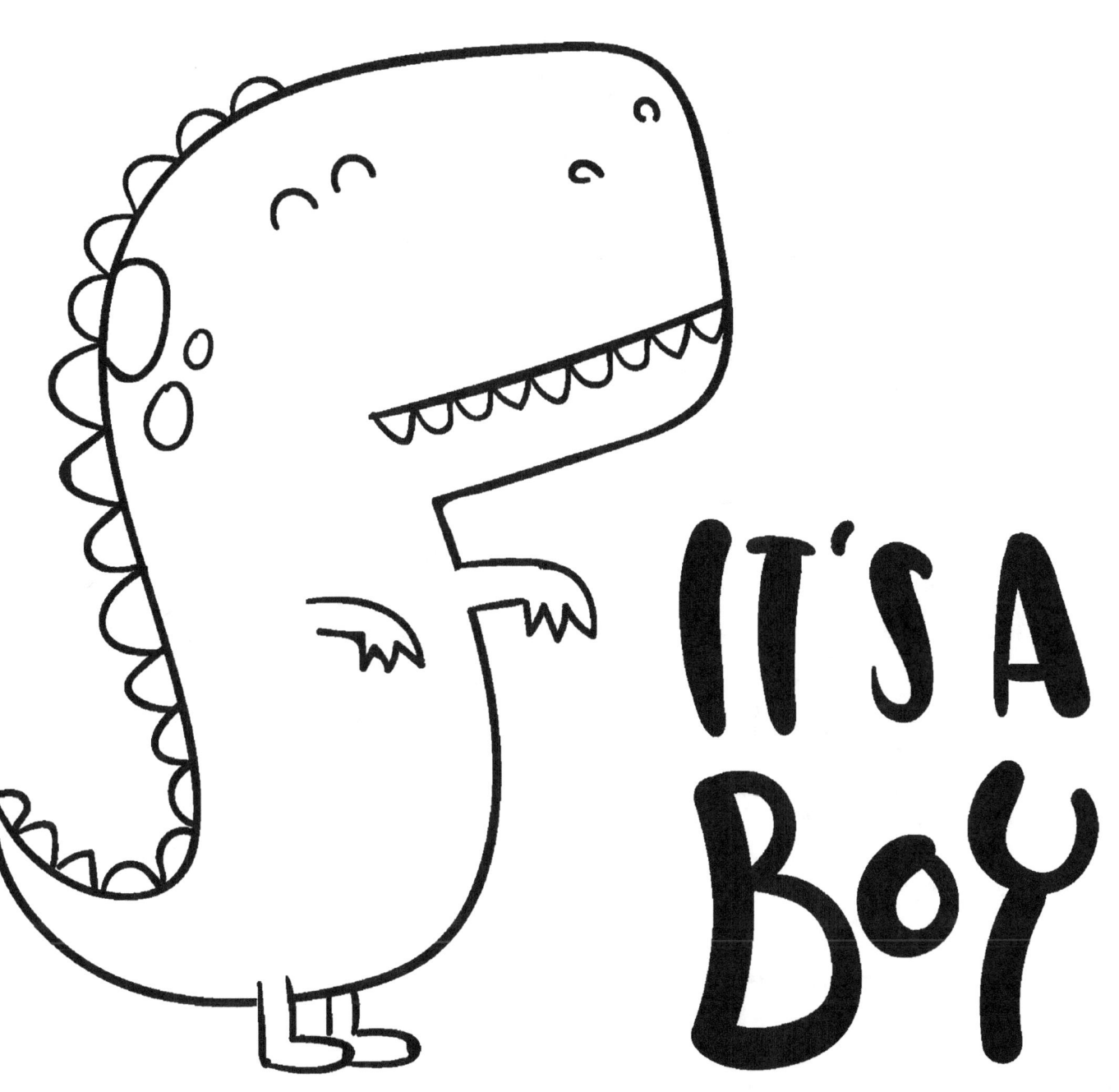

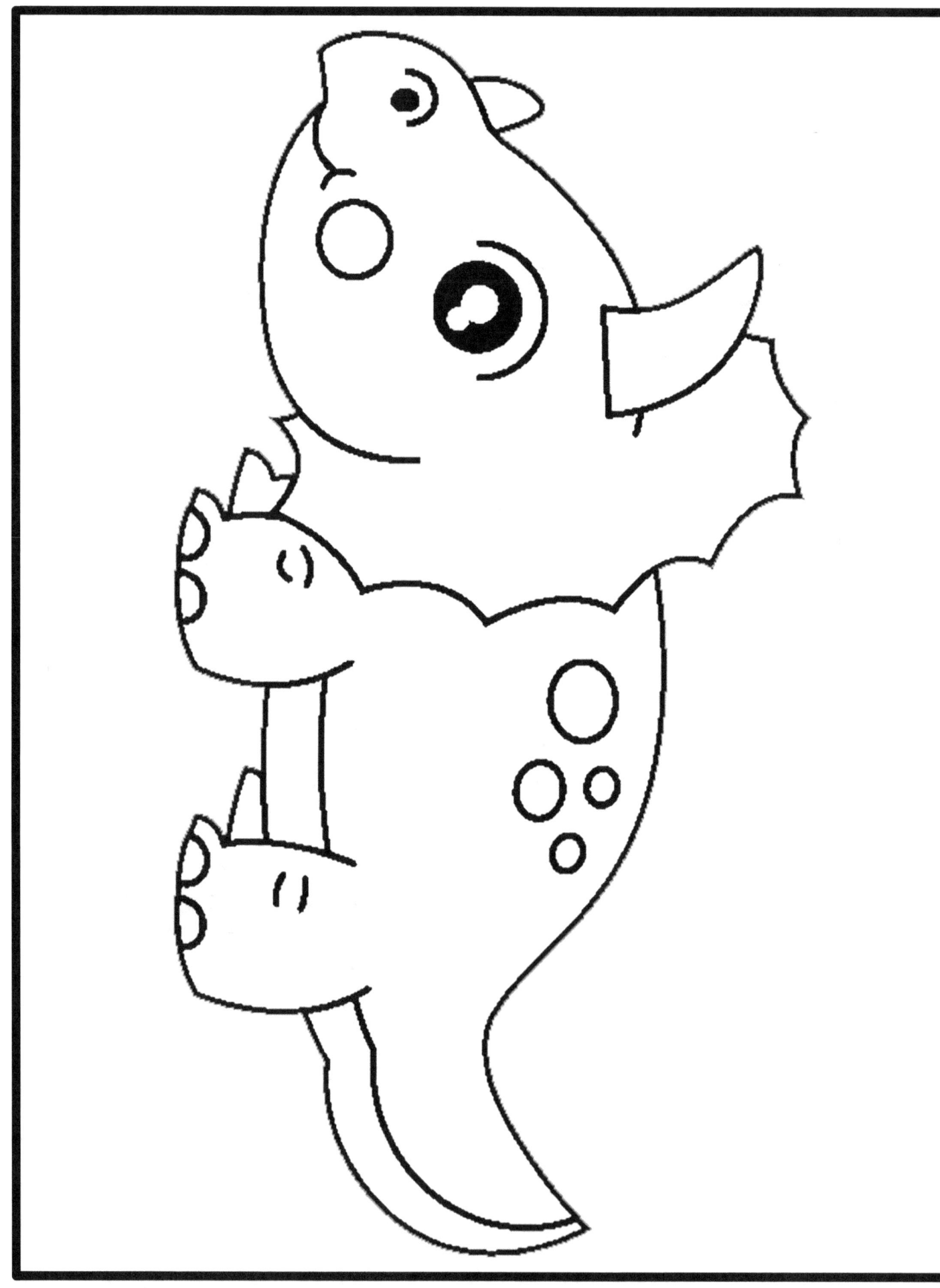

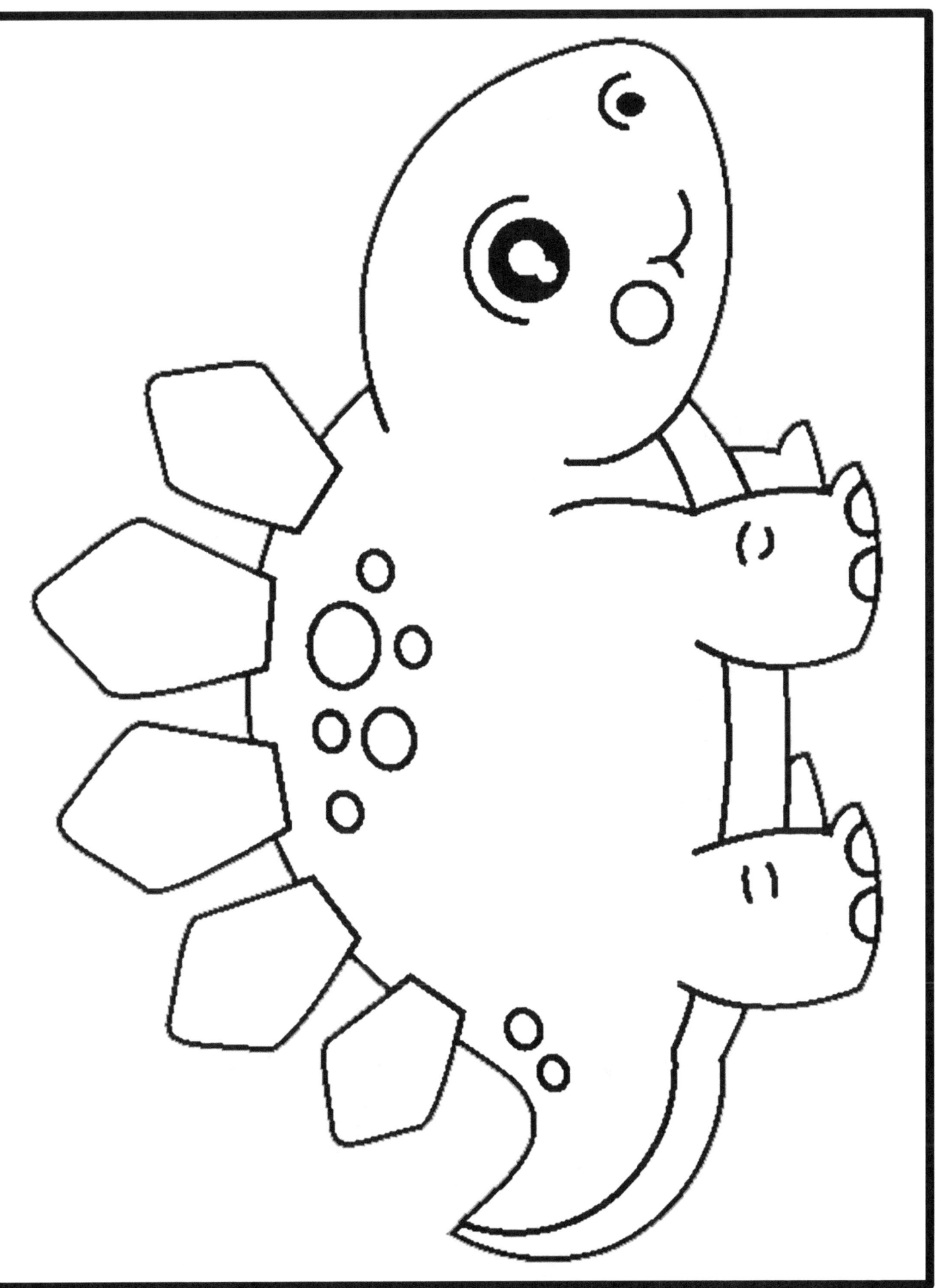

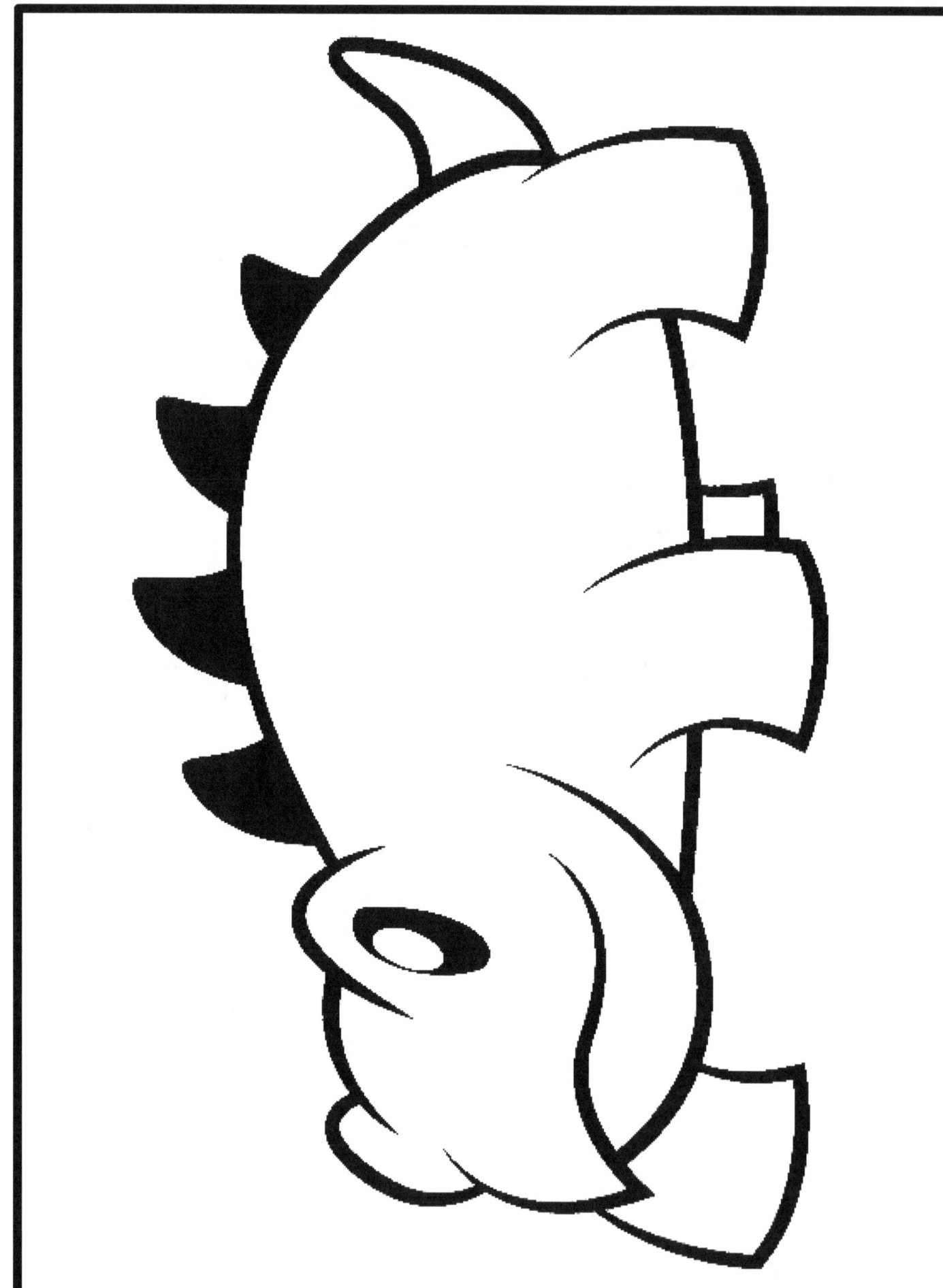

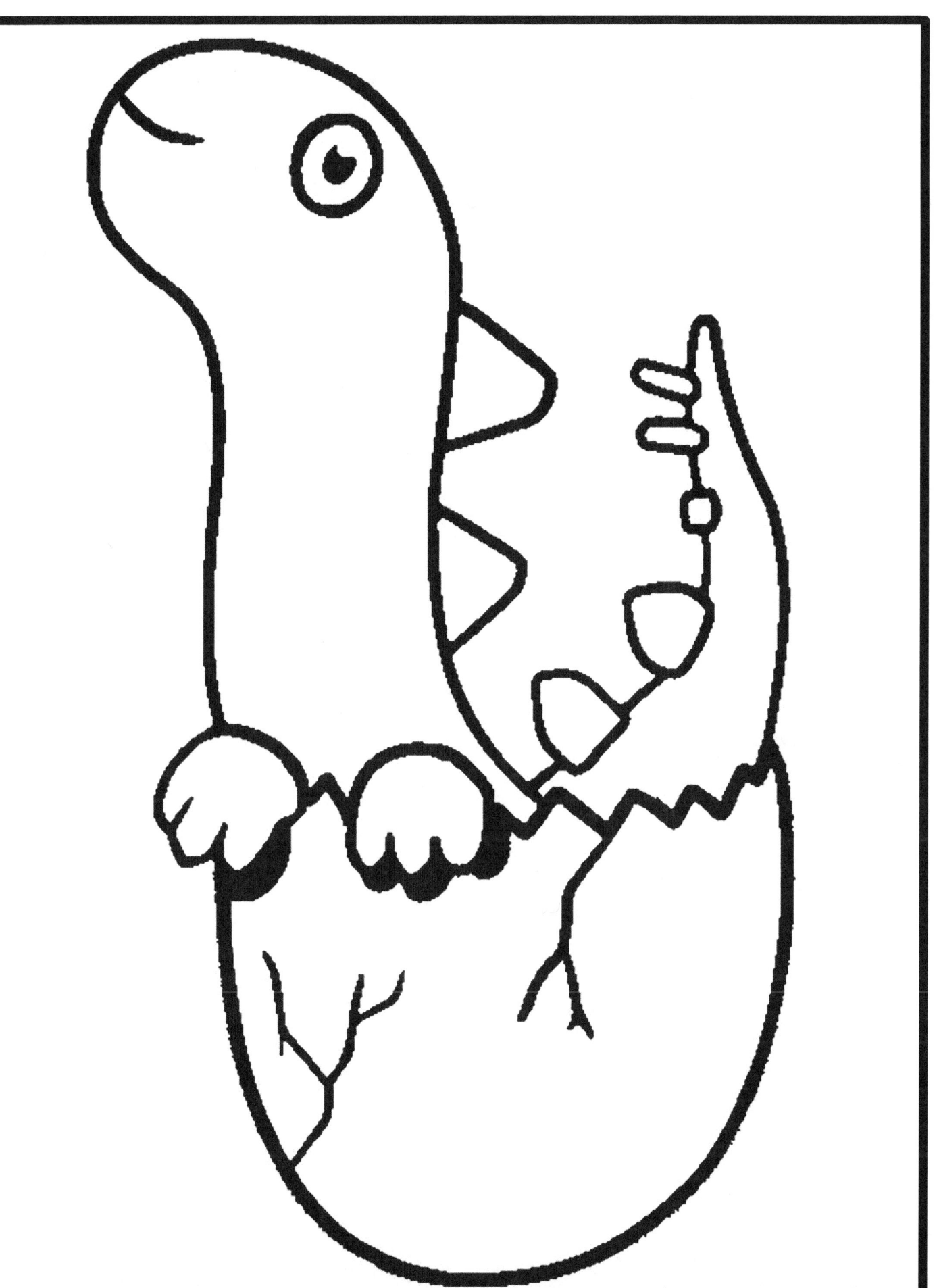

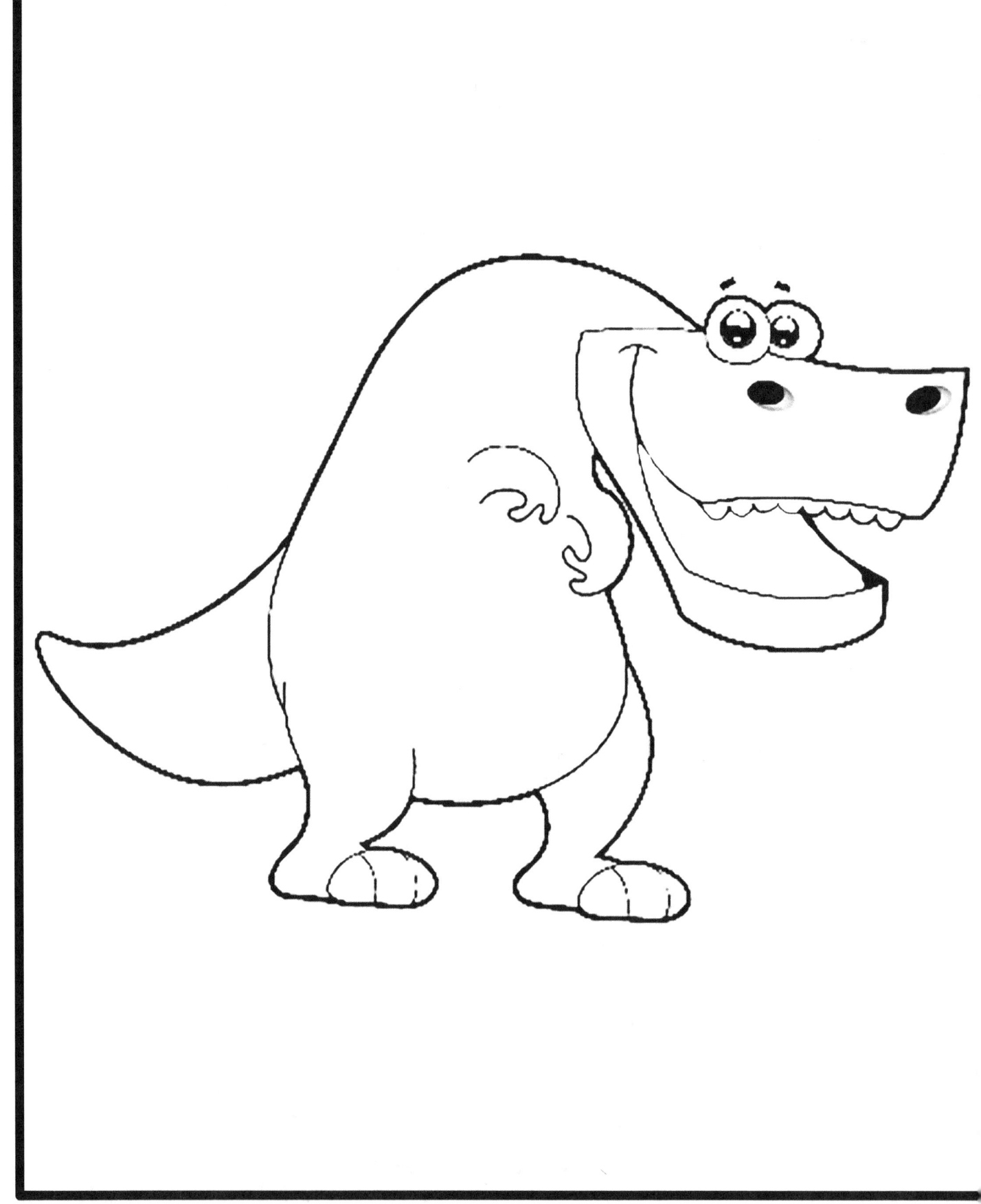

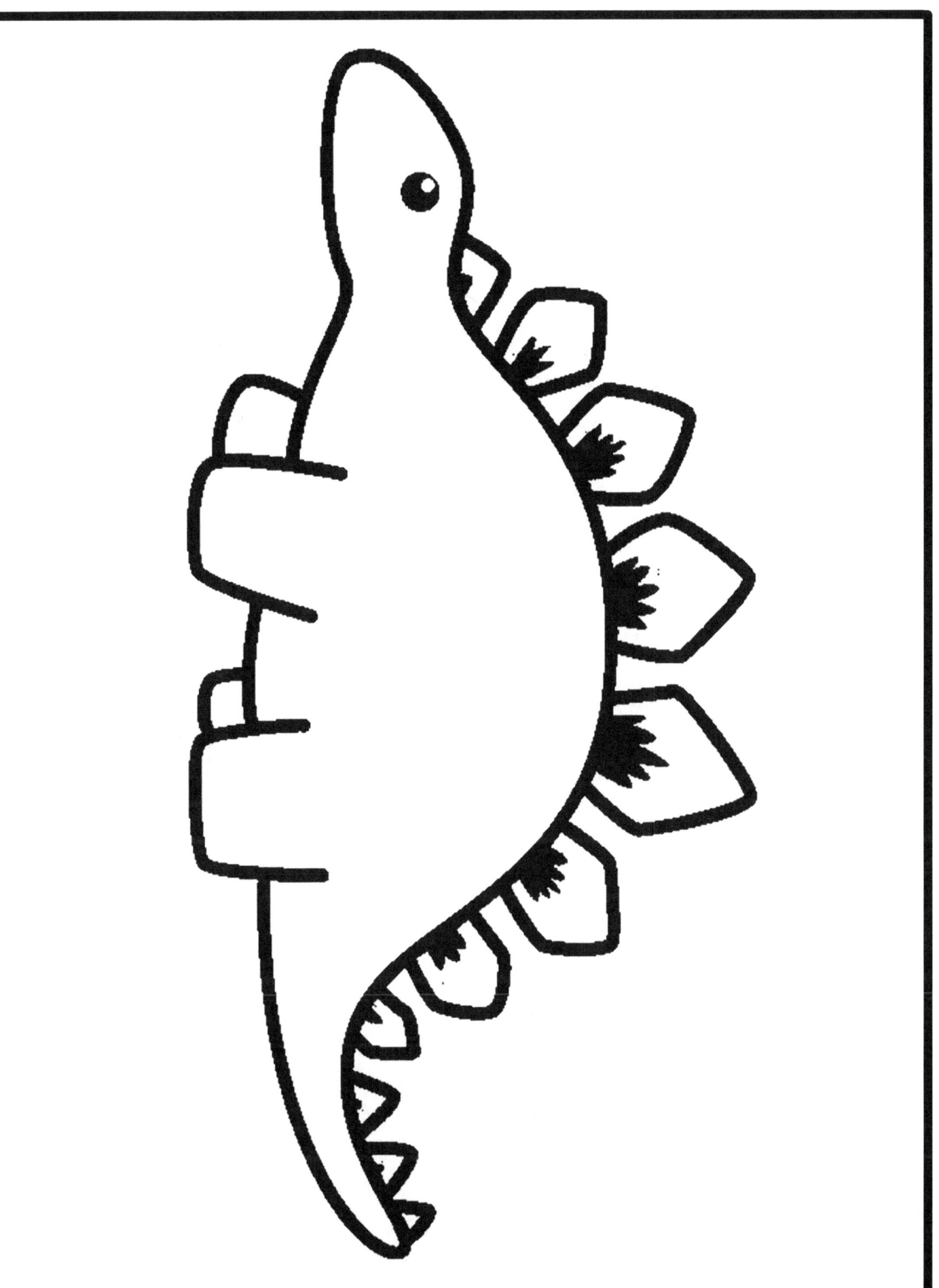

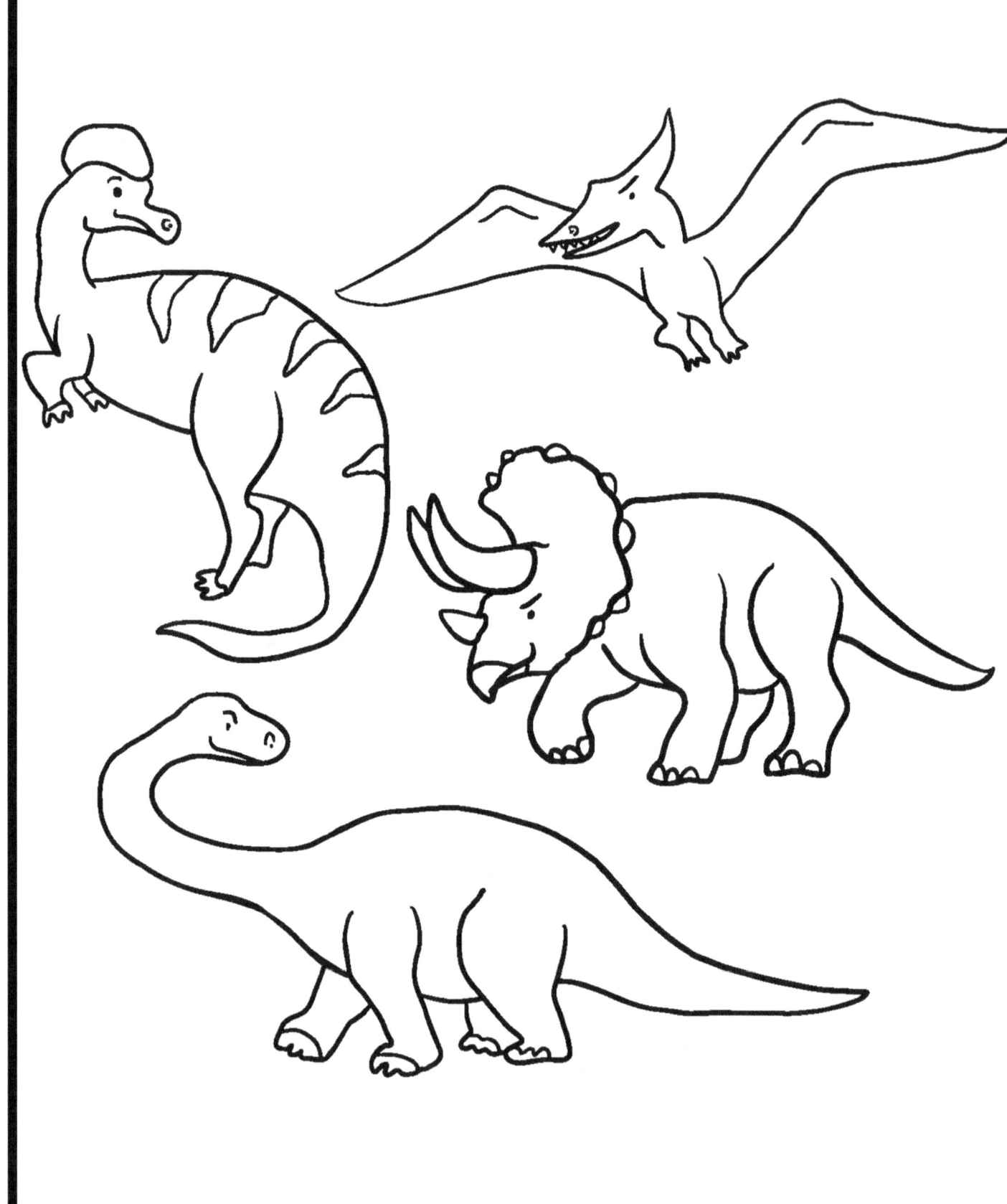

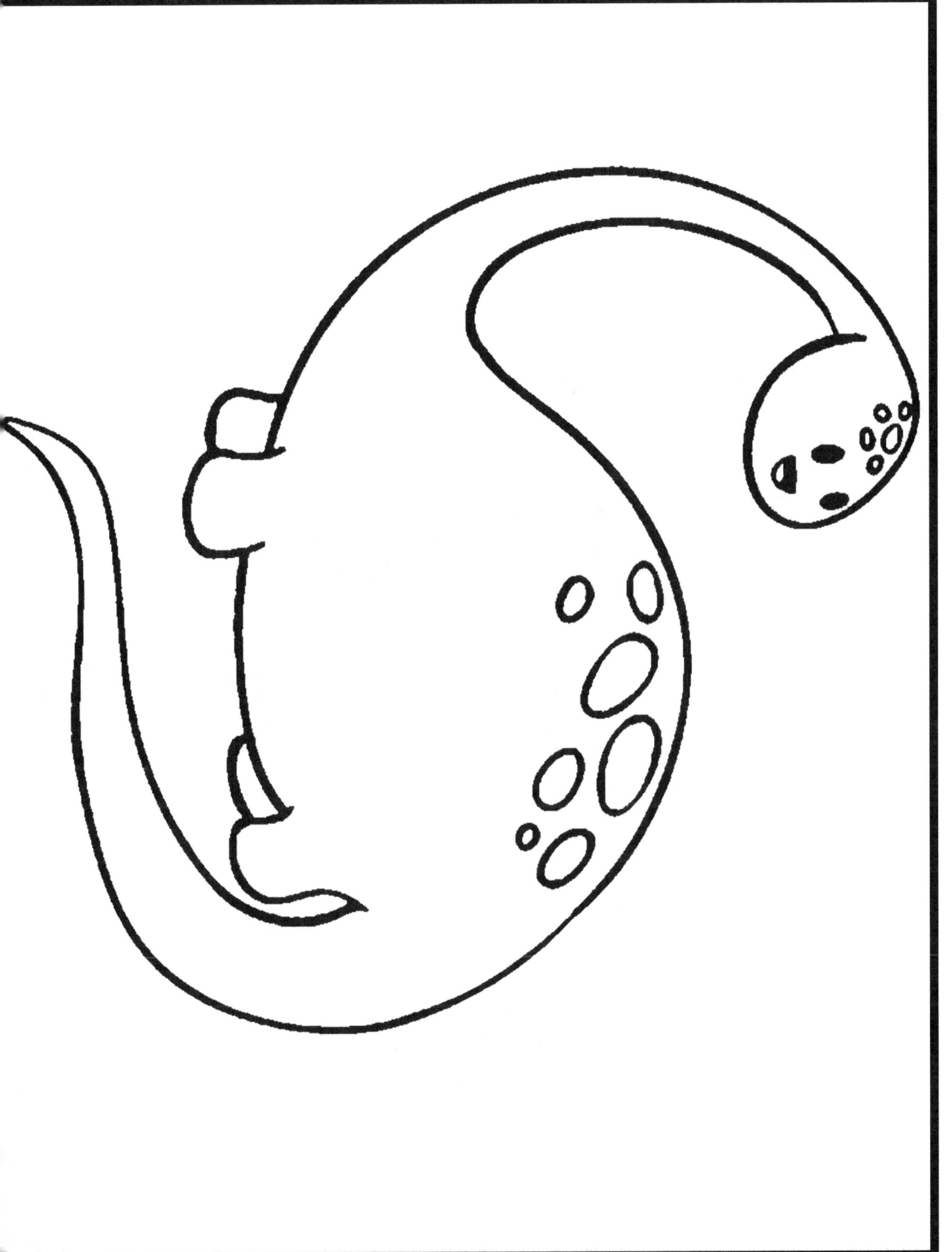

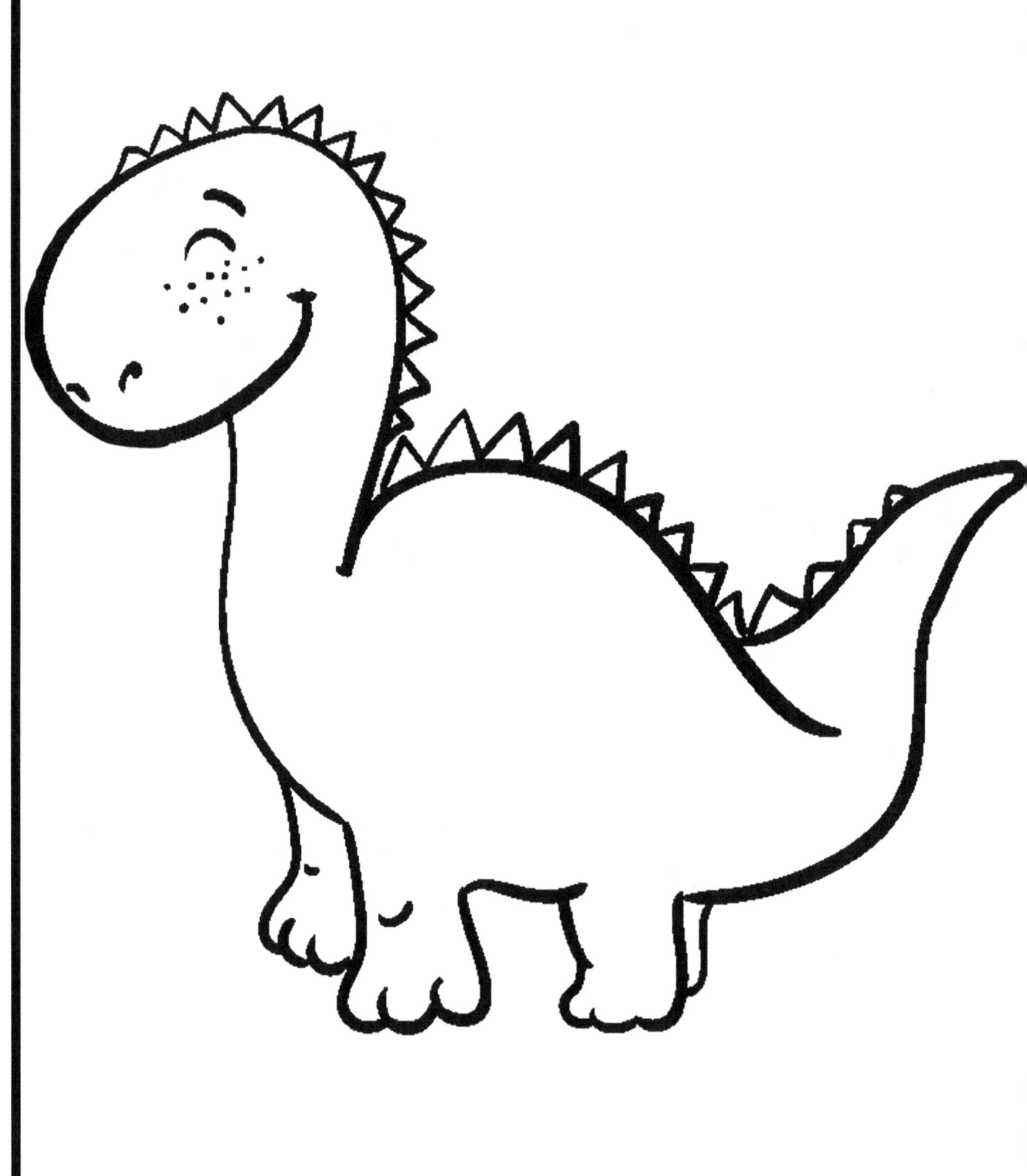

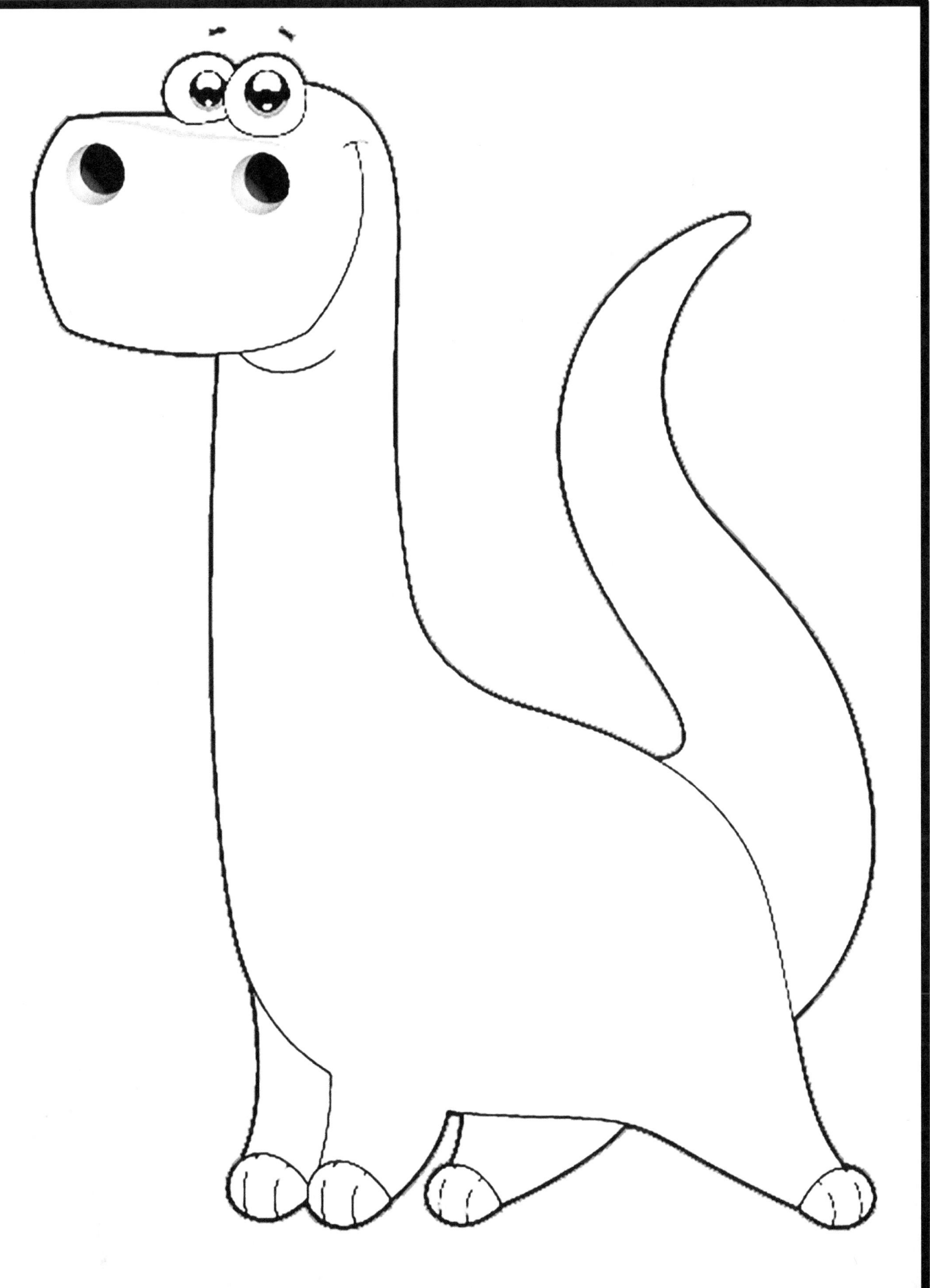

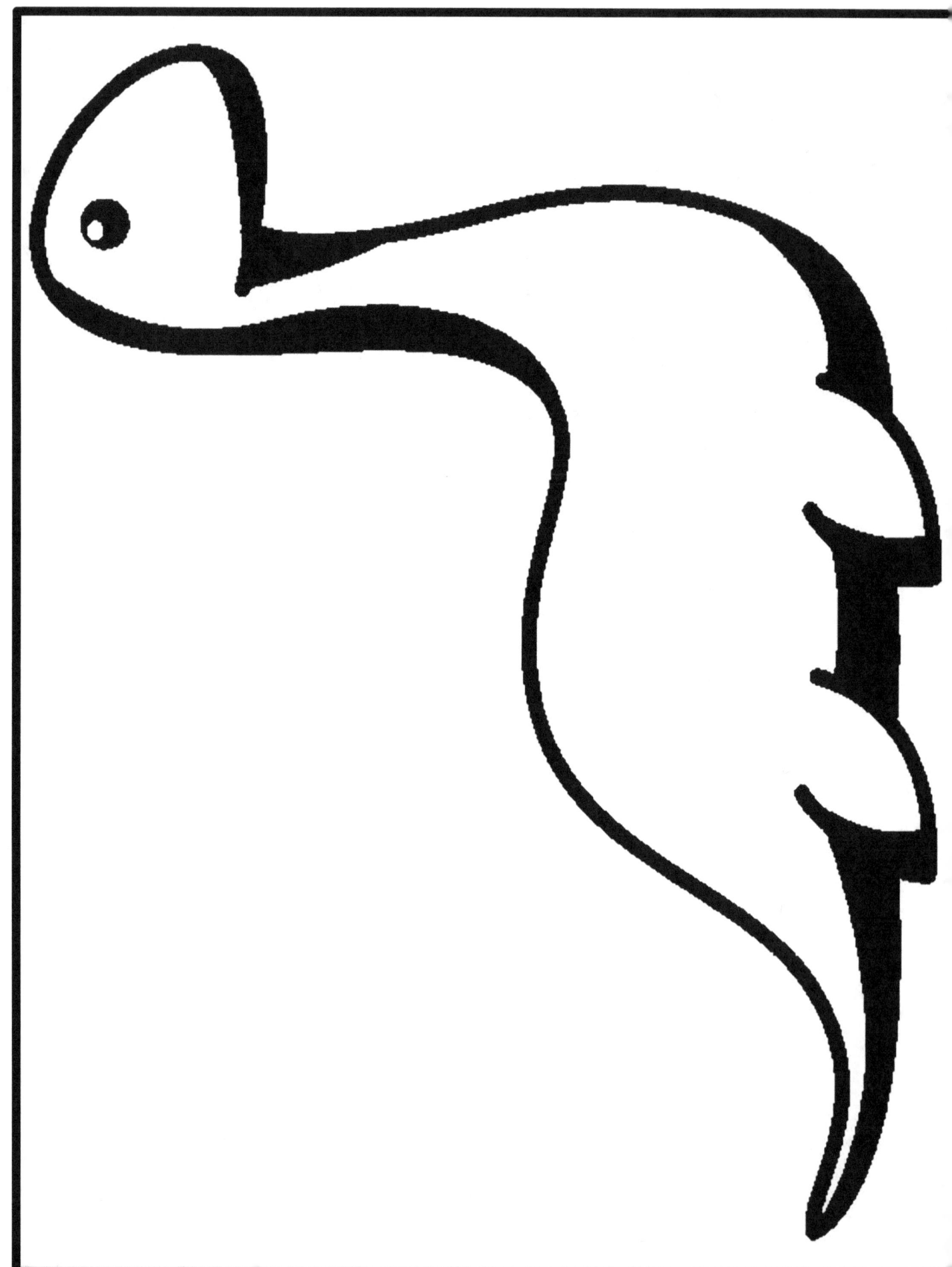

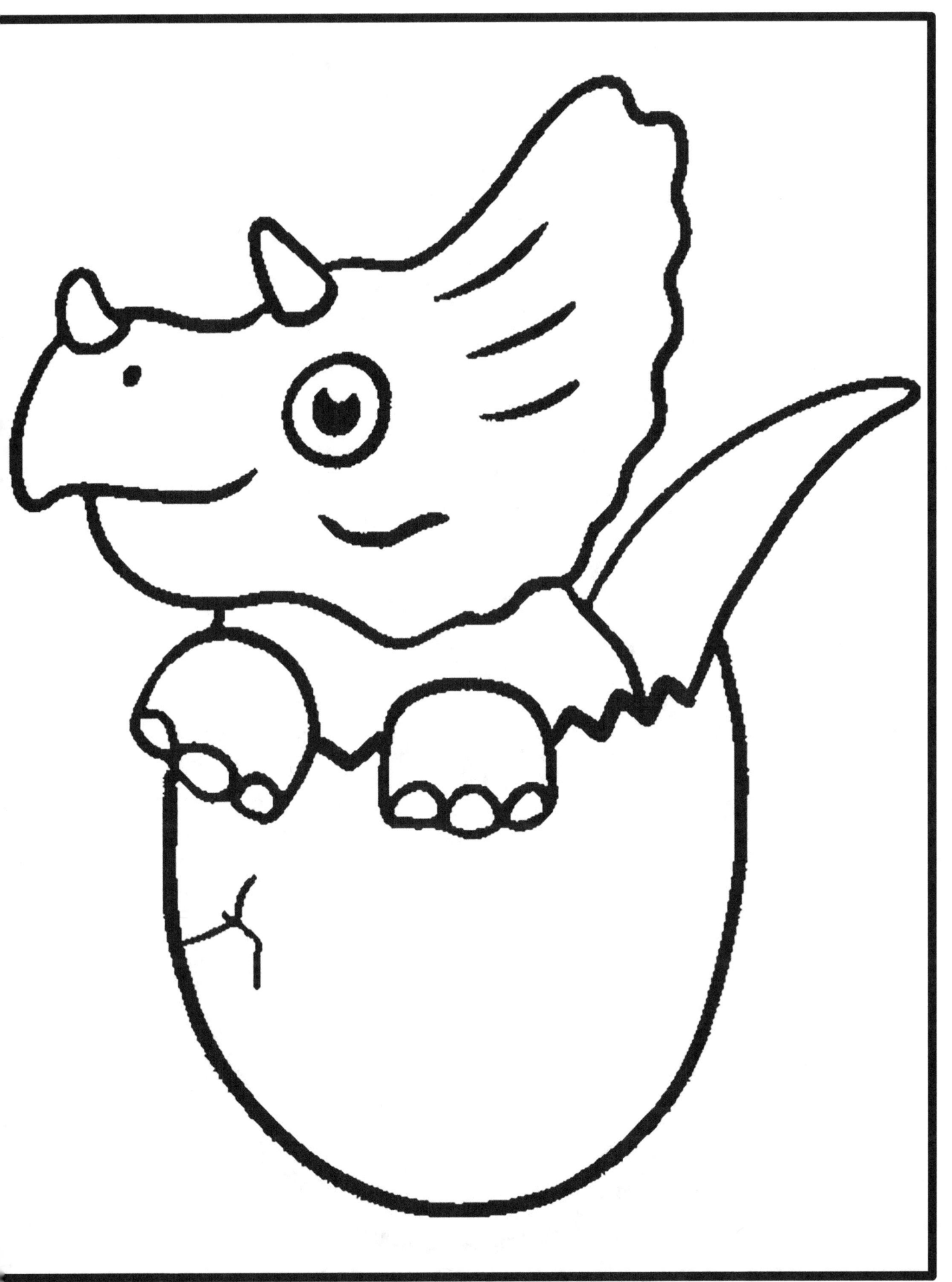

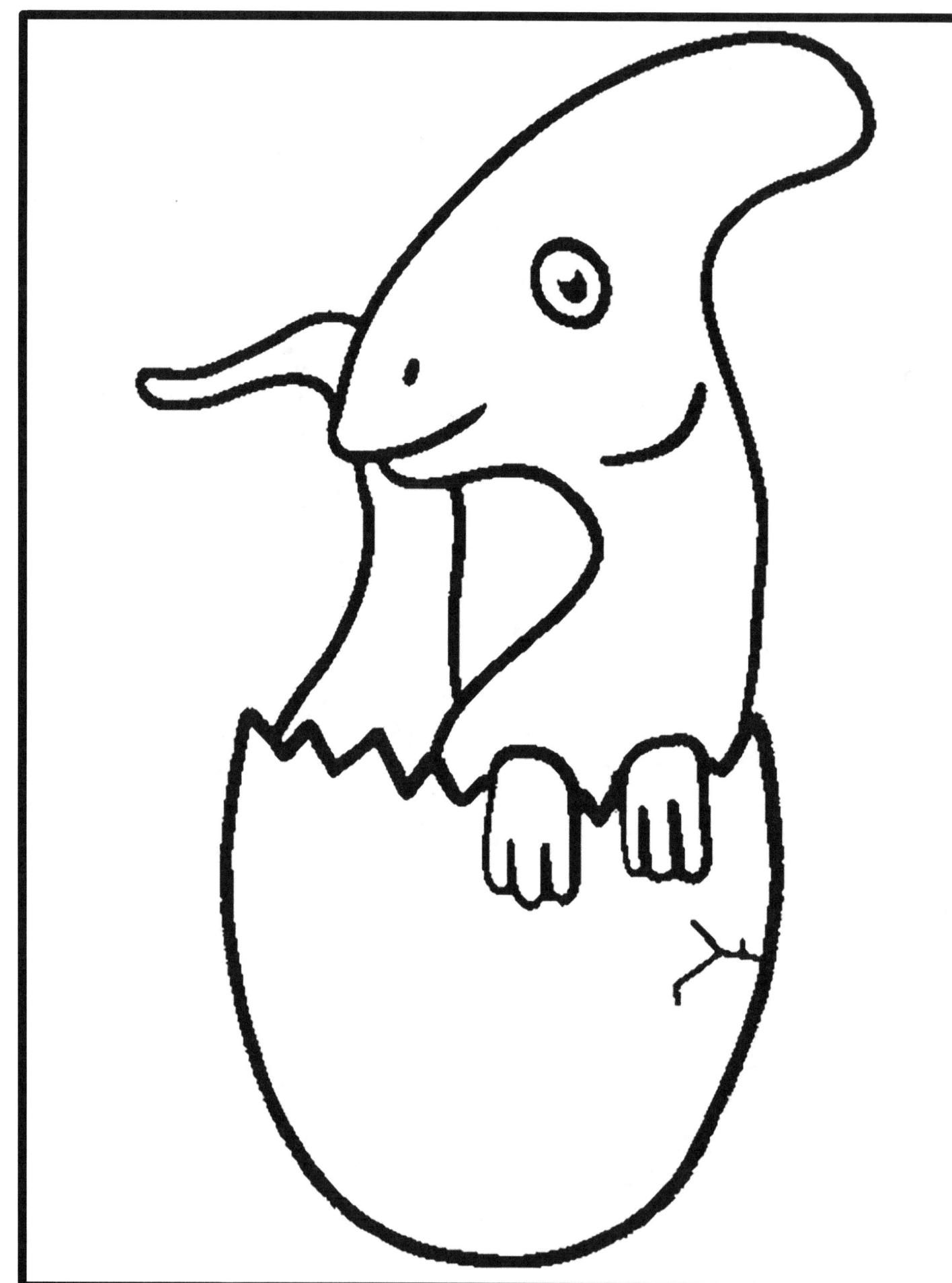

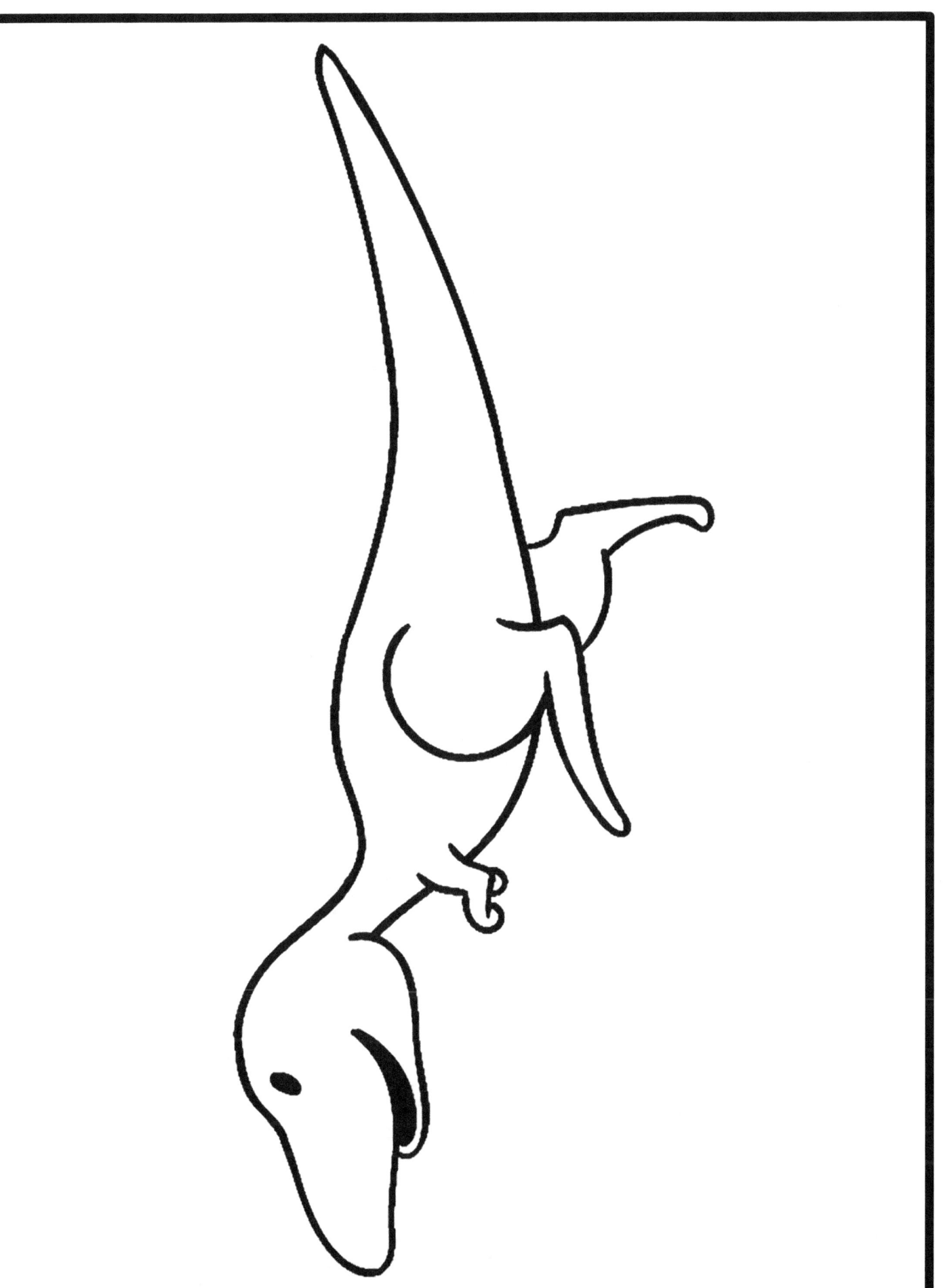

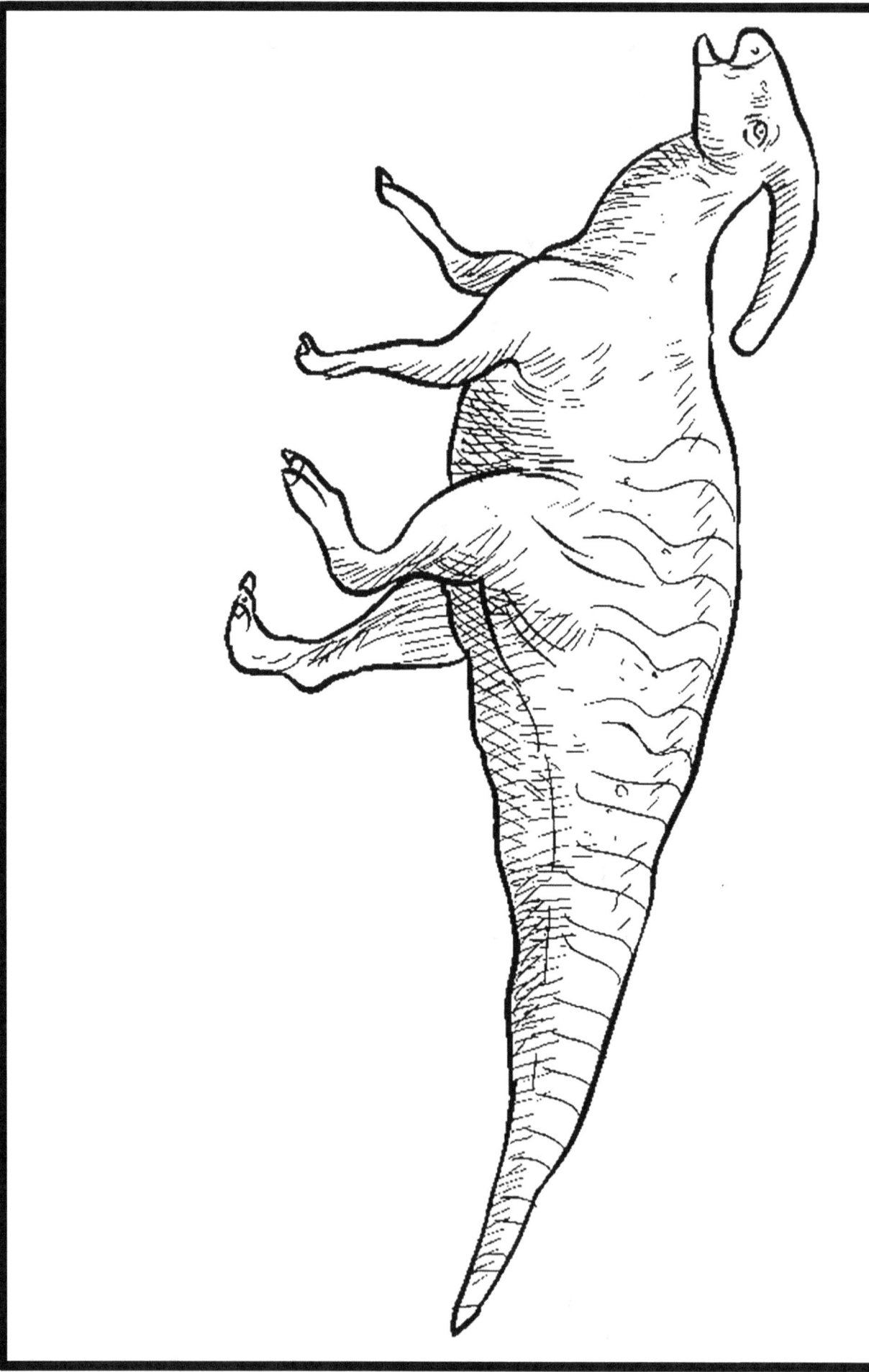

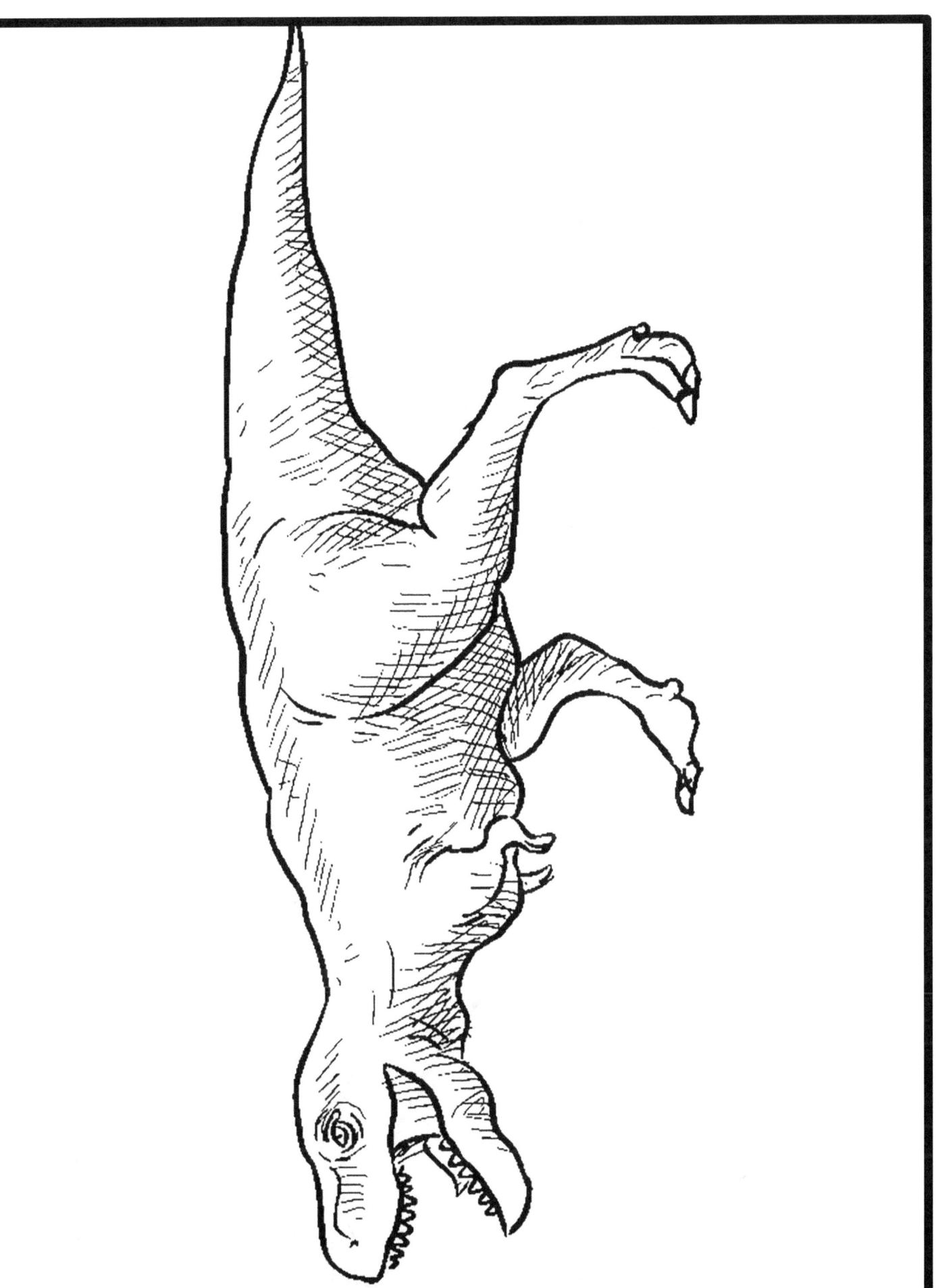

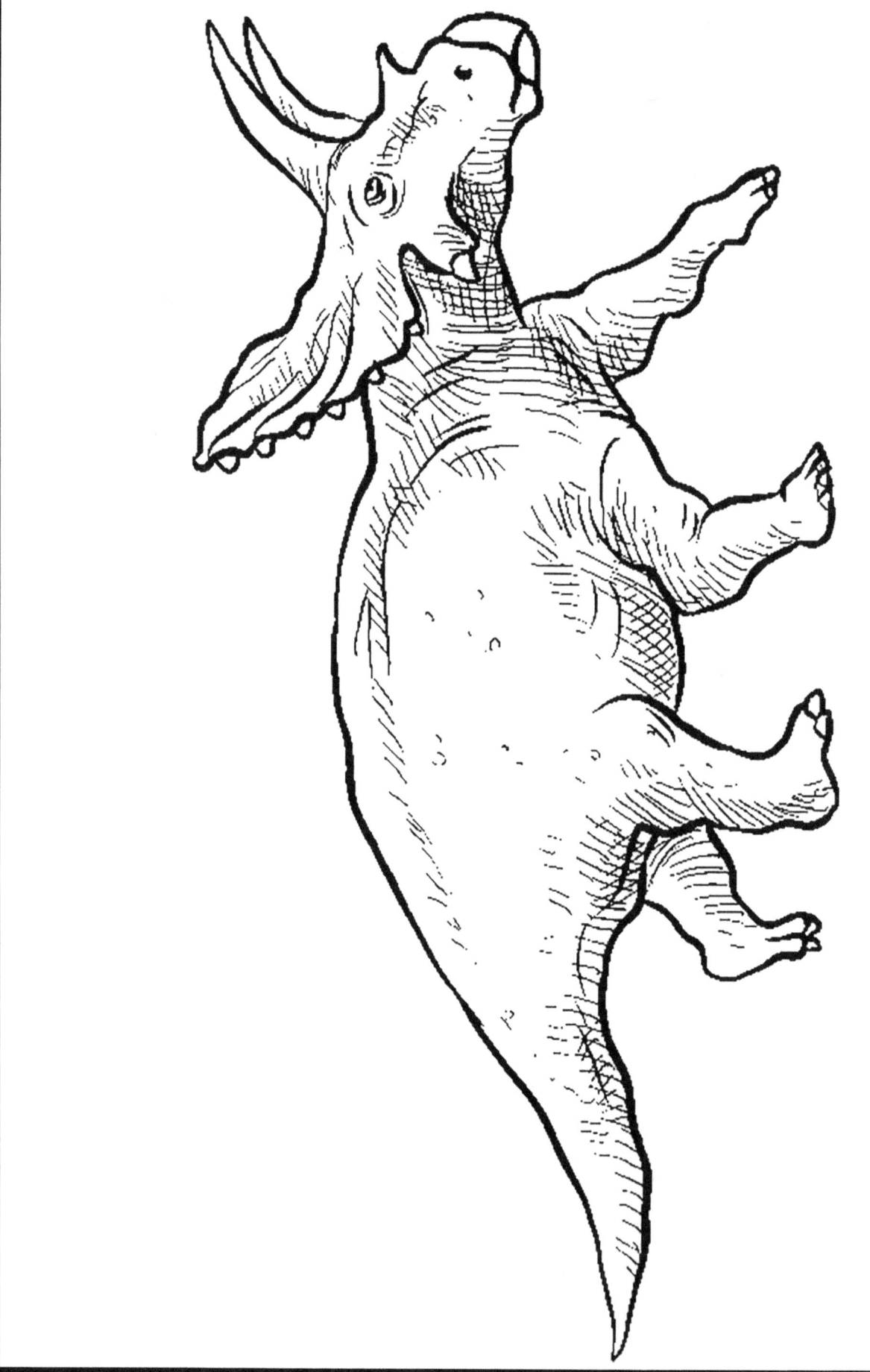

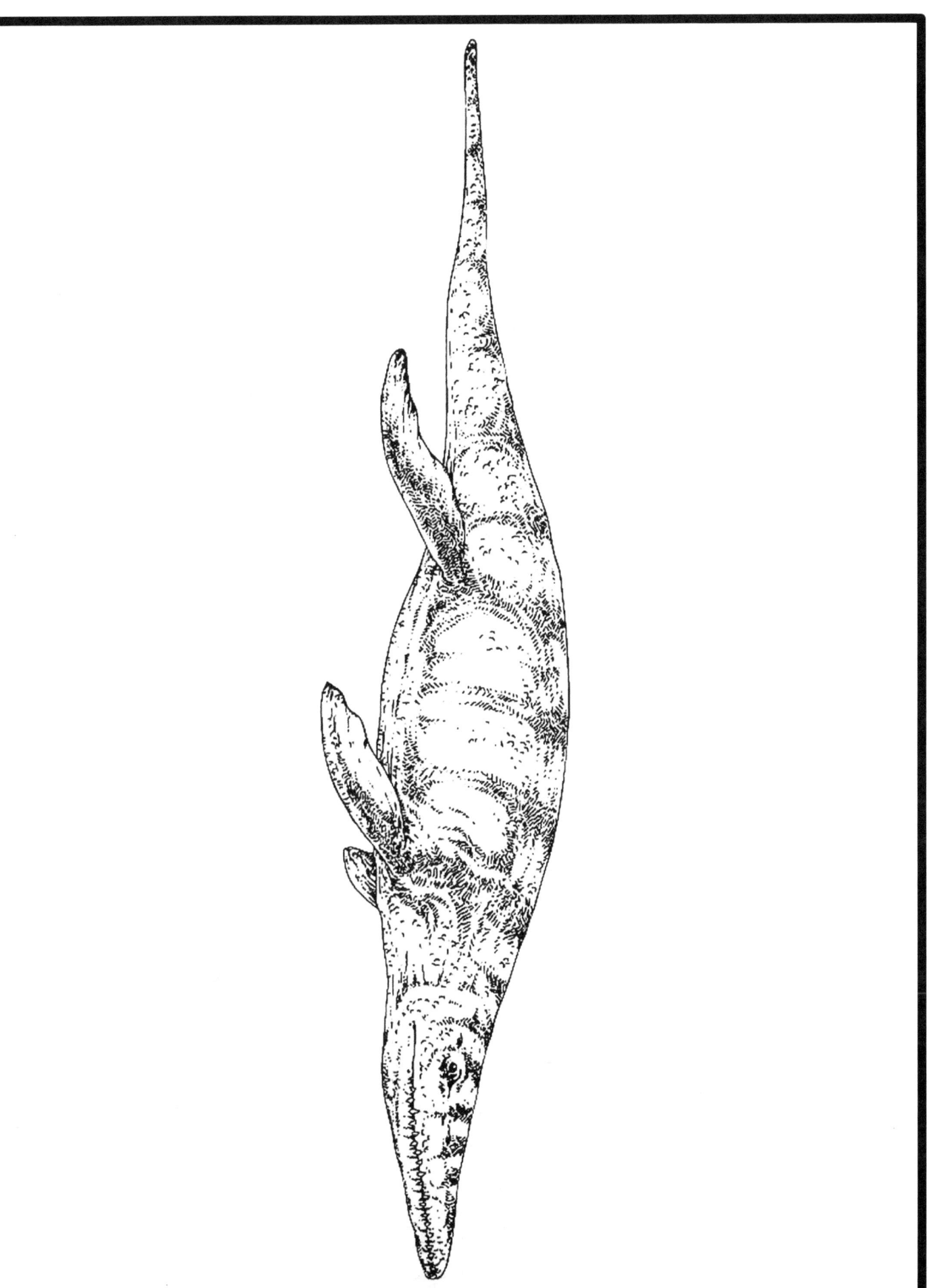

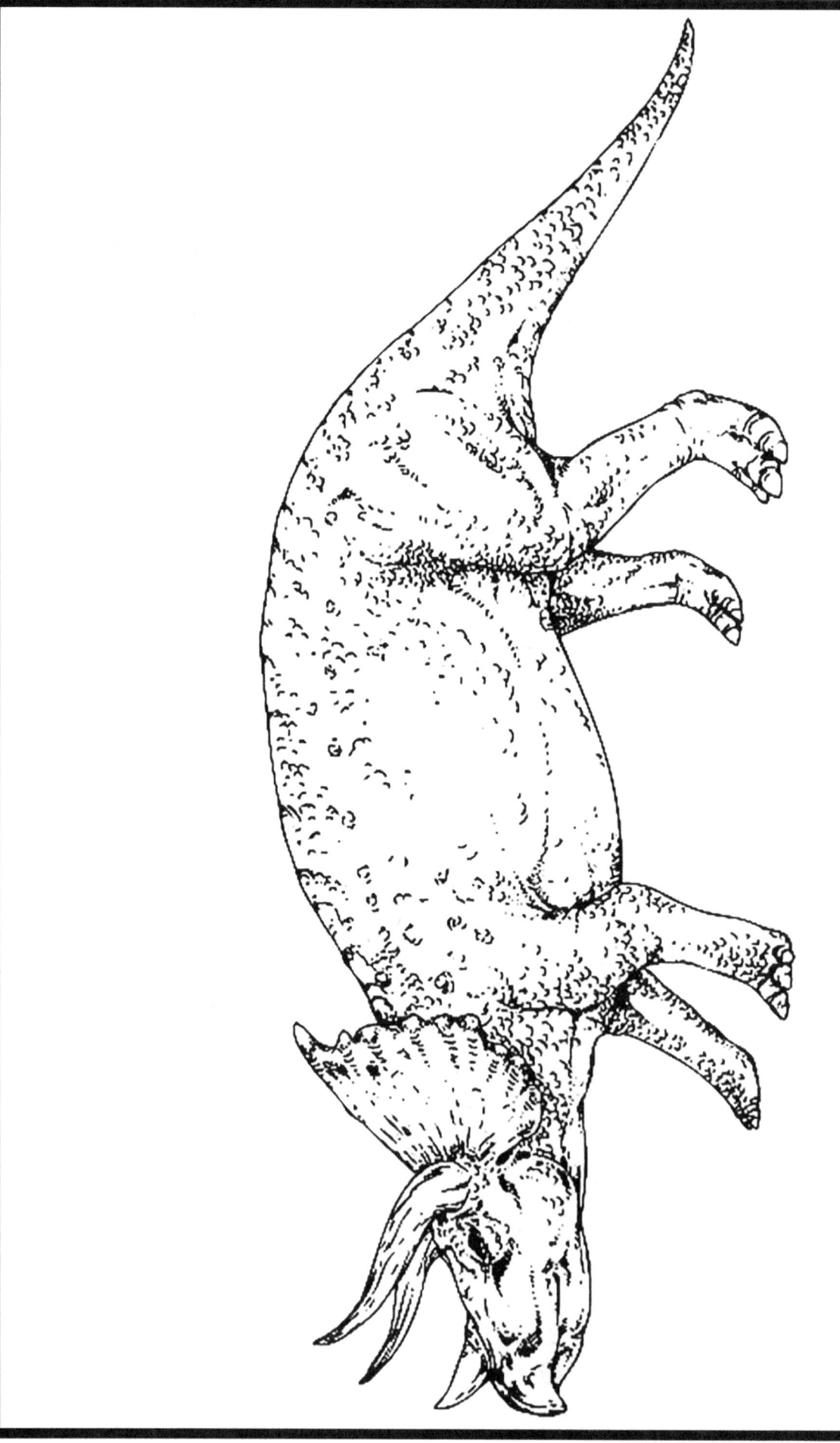

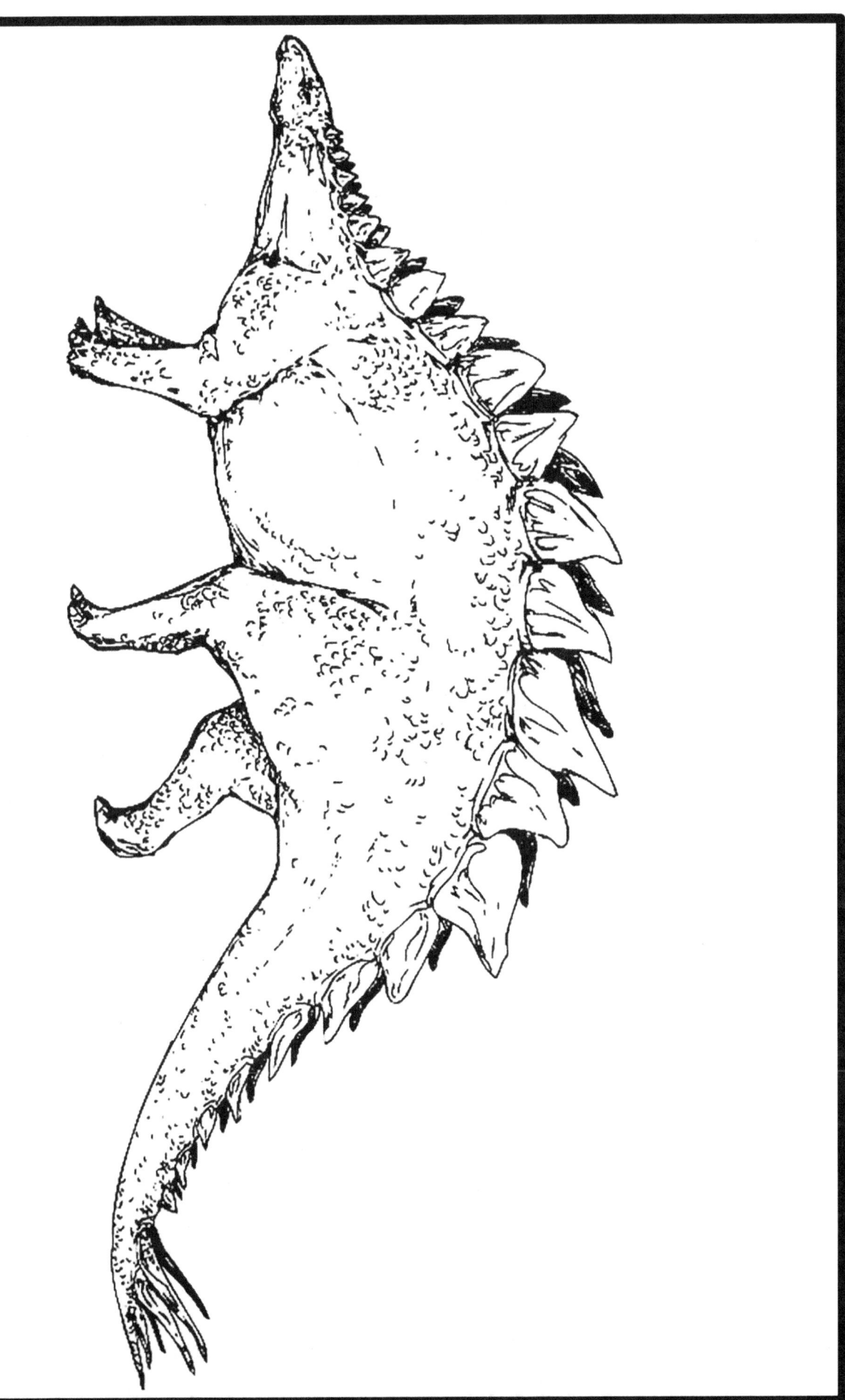

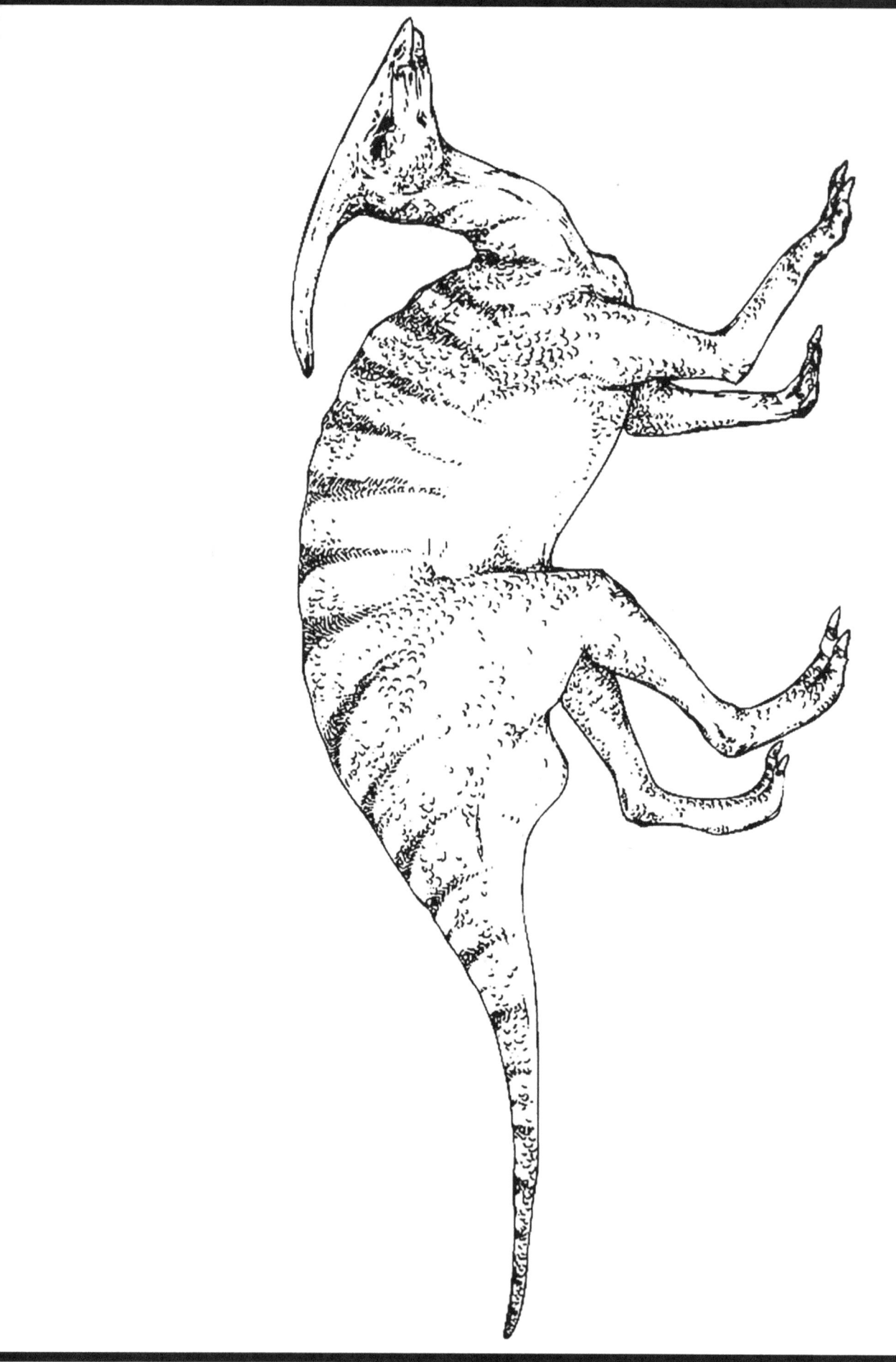

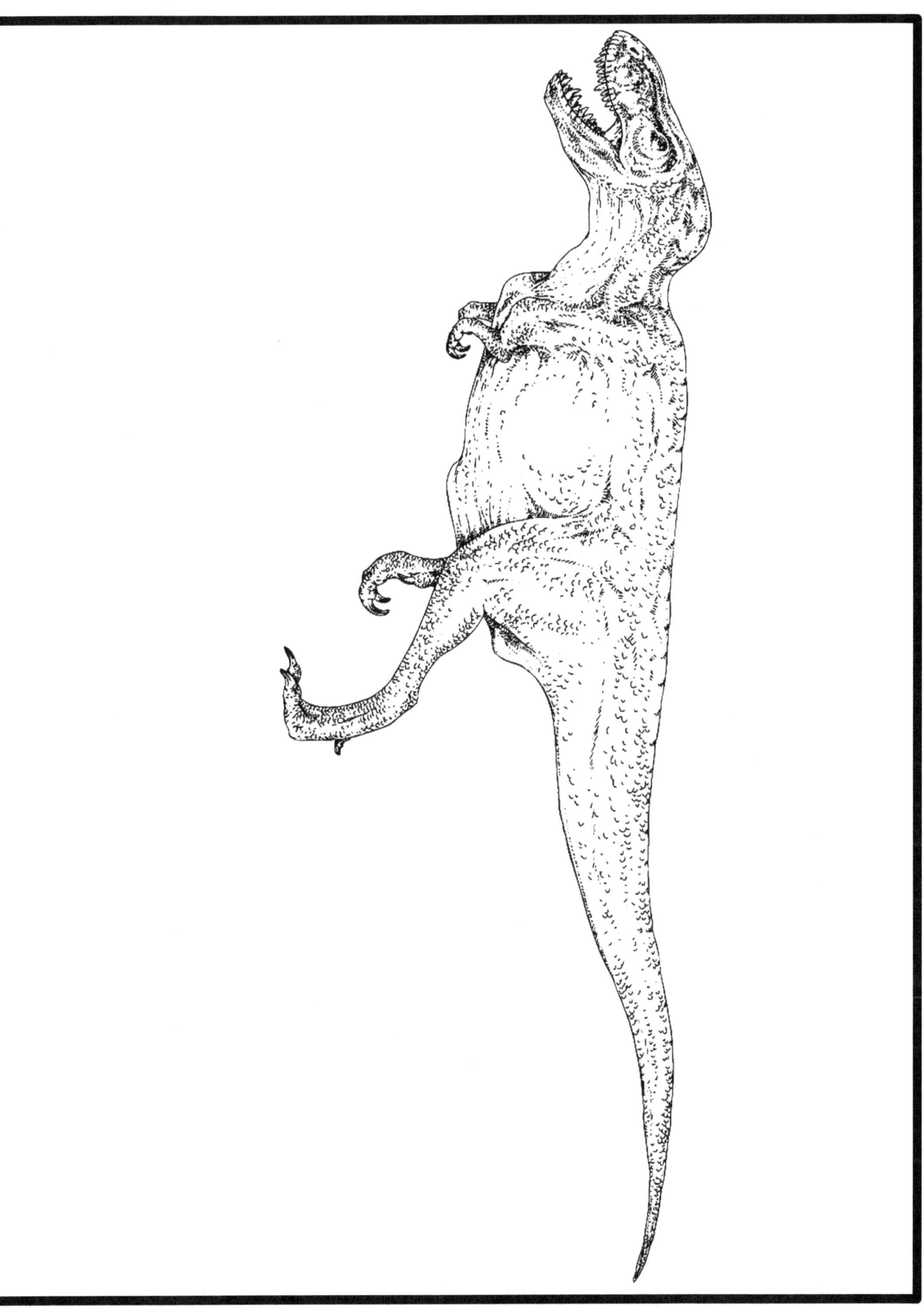

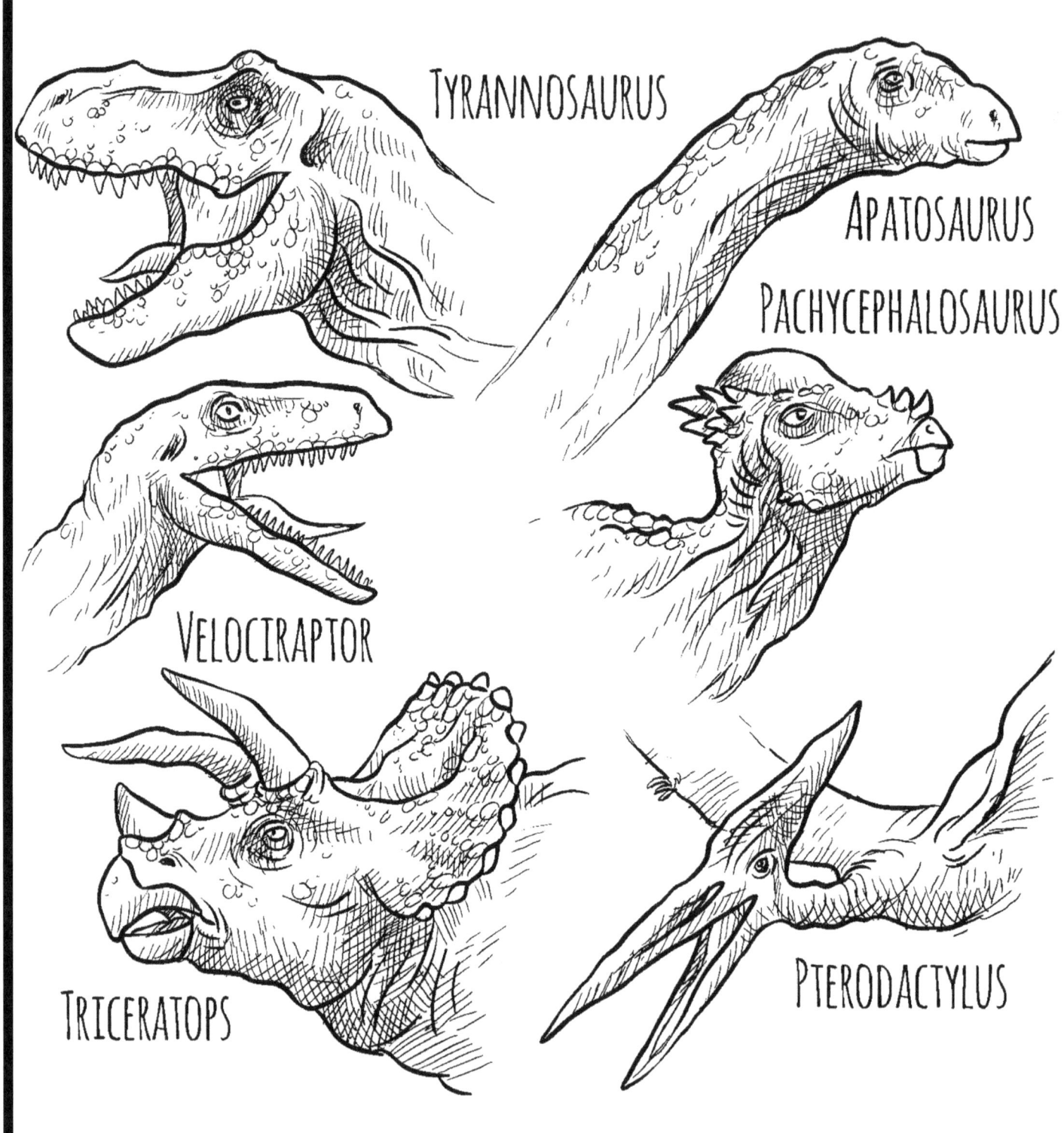

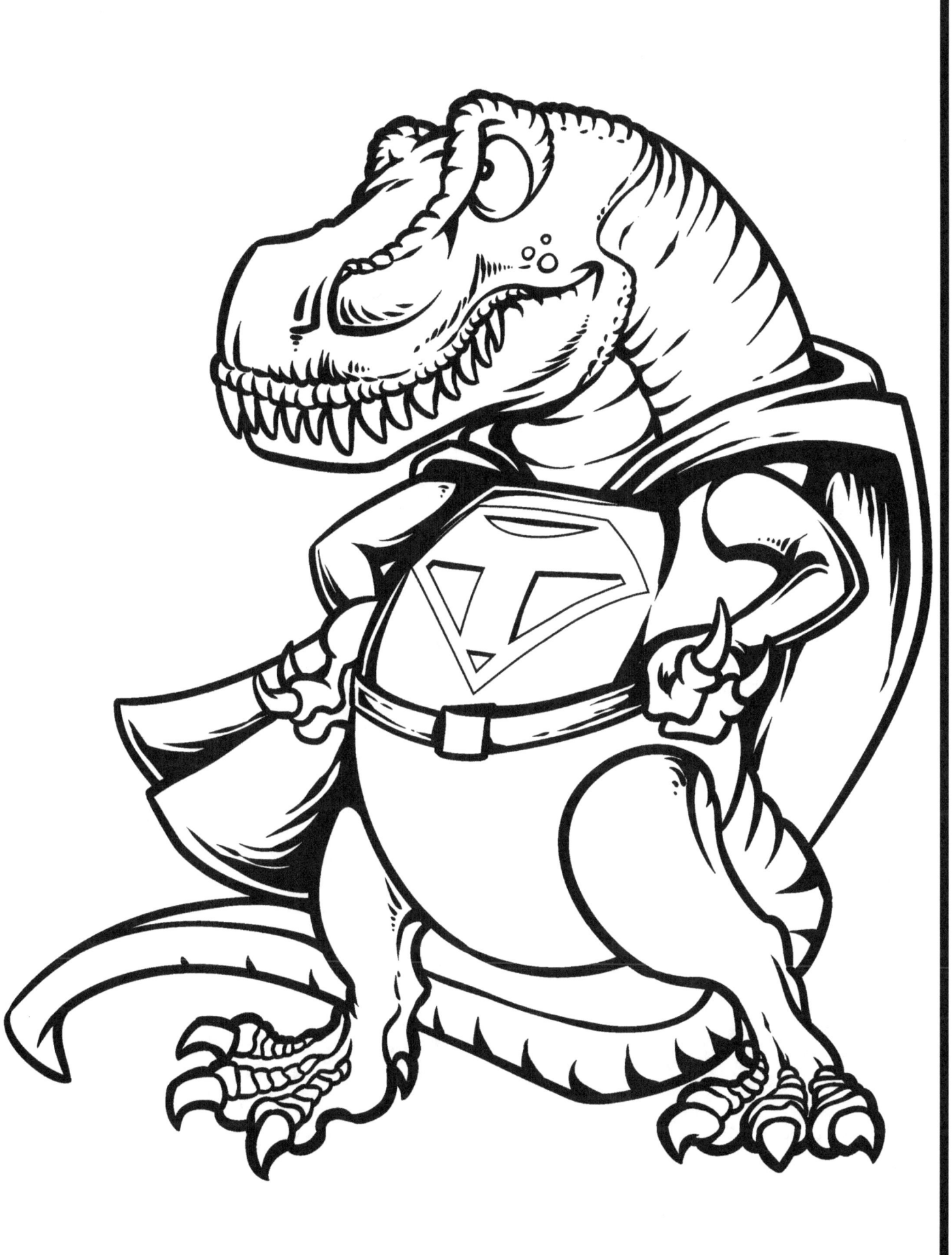

www.ingramcontent.com/pod-product-compliance
Lightning Source LLC
Chambersburg PA
CBHW060004230526
45472CB00008B/1947